THE POWER OF
CORPORATE
KINETICS

CREATE THE SELF-ADAPTING, SELF-RENEWING, INSTANT-ACTION ENTERPRISE

MICHAEL FRADETTE

AND STEVE MICHAUD

A Touchstone Book
Published by SIMON & SCHUSTER

New York   London   Toronto   Sydney   Singapore

TOUCHSTONE
Rockefeller Center
1230 Avenue of the Americas
New York, NY 10020

TOUCHSTONE and colophon are registered trademarks
of Simon & Schuster, Inc.

Designed by Deirdre Amthor

Manufactured in the United States of America

10   9   8   7   6   5   4   3   2   1

The Library of Congress has cataloged the Simon & Schuster edition
as follows:

Fradette, Michael.
The power of corporate kinetics : create the self-adapting, self-renewing,
instant-action enterprise / Michael Fradette and Steve Michaud.
p.   cm.
Includes bibliographical references and index.
1. Management.   2. Organizational change.   3. Adaptability
(Psychology)   I. Michaud, Steve.   II. Title.
HD31.F66   1998
658—dc21   98-16469
CIP

ISBN 0-684-83221-6
0-684-85590-9 (Pbk)

I'd like to dedicate this book first to Debby, my wife, for her unwavering support and selflessness in making the family work in my absences; and to my daughters, Nicole and Jacquelyn, for their individual inspirations to me to reach for something special inside all of us.

M.F.

To my wife, Donna, and my children, Tyler, Trevor, Alison, and Ashley, without whose support and devotion I could never have practiced my profession long enough to acquire the experiences necessary to write this book.

S.M.

From both of us, to our colleagues at Deloitte Consulting, who, without their insight, collaboration, and support, this book would not be possible.

We're in a brawl with no rules.

—PAUL A. ALLAIRE, CHAIRMAN AND
CEO, XEROX CORPORATION

If you're not confused, you don't know what's going on.

—JOHN F. WELCH, JR., CHAIRMAN
AND CEO, GENERAL ELECTRIC
COMPANY

Only the productive survive.

—ANDREW S. GROVE, CHAIRMAN
AND CEO, INTEL CORPORATION

ACKNOWLEDGMENTS

In 1995, a team of frontline Deloitte Consulting partners—each representing a different industry and a different business discipline—came together to examine and understand a fundamental shift they were observing among pioneering companies. It quickly became evident that this new approach to business was not isolated to one industry or one kind of company. *The Power of Corporate Kinetics* is the culmination of the insights and discoveries from this team's two-year exploration. The initiative was not appointed by any leader but grew out of the passion of frontline workers who saw a discontinuity in the marketplace and organized themselves to champion a discovery and solutions that would allow enterprises everywhere to succeed in a radically changing world. It was kinetics in action.

We would like to thank our colleagues who were willing to lead from the front line of our business and assisted us:

Richard Shafer, Ph.D., on people and agility. (A partner when our project began, Dick is now director of executive education at Cornell University's School of Industrial and Labor Relations. He has contributed his personal research and insights on kinetic leaders and workers to give us a complete picture of the kinetic enterprise.)

Cheryl Robbins on the health care industry and on operations and process design.

Steven Baldwin on the process manufacturing industry and on operations management.

James Haines on the discrete manufacturing industry and strategy.

John Namovic on the telecommunications and media industry.

Peter Gertler on consumer products manufacturers, distributors and retailers, and electronic commerce.

Jeff Farin on the financial services industry.

Douglas Lattner on the energy industry.

Robert Campbell on the public sector.

Mel Lewis on technology.

We are also grateful to members of our team who helped us turn our frontline insights into a form that could be shared with everyone: Terry Ribb, who championed the learning and book development process, and without whose unyielding and tireless commitment this book would never have been completed; the writers and editors at Wordworks, Inc.—Christina Braun, Donna Sammons Carpenter, Maurice Coyle, Erik Hansen, Martha Lawler, Cindy Sammons, Bob Stock, Sebastian Stuart, Saul Wisnia, and Pat Wright—who brought their expertise to this project; Helen Rees, our literary agent, who made global publication possible; and Fred Hills of Simon & Schuster, who believed in kinetics and helped us each step of the way.

CONTENTS

PART 1

THE DESTINATION

EMBRACE THE POWER OF
CORPORATE KINETICS

INTRODUCTION

MANY a forest has been felled of late to print the avalanche of books and articles advising us how to fix up and make over our organizations. Whatever your views of this outpouring, we believe it is no accident. It is a visceral response to the feelings of confusion and uncertainty that have arisen in our corporate lives. The business world, swept by technological and geopolitical changes, plagued by concern over an unknown and unpredictable future, is looking for answers.

Most of the suggestions and plans offered to date have focused on cutting costs, trimming staffs, reengineering processes, and the like. They have accepted as a given the essential organizational model that has governed corporations for generations. We believe that the challenges we now face are of a whole new order of magnitude and demand a comparable response. In this book we point the way toward a new model of the business enterprise—its strategic stance, its processes, its workforce, and its leadership.

We invite you to join us on a journey toward what we call a kinetic enterprise, which is both a vision and a reality: a vision because no organization today has fully realized the potential of this approach; a reality because many leading enterprises have adopted one or more of its underlying principles.

We have divided the book into two parts. In Part 1 we set forth the principles and attributes of the kinetic enterprise. In Part 2 we offer practical suggestions and case histories to show

how the new model can be implemented, with an emphasis on the dramatically different role of the enterprise's leadership team.

But first, let us suggest something of what is to follow, in the form of the two outrageous goals of the kinetic enterprise— spurs to drive us toward a future in which we will have learned to cope with the sudden jolts and discontinuities of a drastically new business environment.

1. *Serve a single customer.* Provide the sales relationships, products, and services to match the infinitely diverse and changing demands of individual customers, one by one.

2. *Act in zero time.* Meet customer demands and exploit market opportunities instantly by means of simultaneous enterprise-wide collaborations and action.

In the course of our journey we will be bumping into those goals again and again, in one form or another, as we sketch the portrait of an organization that steadfastly pursues its strategic purposes by constantly shifting and adjusting its perceptions and processes. The road to the kinetic future beckons. Join us in answering the call.

CHAPTER 1

THE DEATH OF PREDICTABILITY

YOU CAN'T PREDICT THE FUTURE, BUT YOU CAN BE READY FOR WHATEVER IT BRINGS

> Kinetics comes from the Greek word *kinesis,* for movement. The dictionary defines kinetic as an adjective "relating to the motion of material bodies and the forces and energy associated therewith." We apply it to a dynamic business that instantly responds to new demands and seizes new opportunities.

SOMETIMES you have to step back from the pressures and challenges of your daily routine and try to make sense of it all. Where is your industry going? What are your company's prospects? Where is your career headed? We believe that you ignore these questions at your peril. All those trees that keep you from seeing the forest have contrived to create a whole new business environment. Something profound has changed: Predictability is dead.

This book is about the death of predictability and how you can turn it to your advantage.

Until now, virtually every work of management theory, as well as every business, has been based on a single premise: The future is predictable. Until now, we have forecast market trends, scheduled production, designed services, and trained employees on the assumption that we could count on a stable future except for the occasional unexpected earthquake.

In one sense, of course, the unexpected is a business staple. In fact, business would be pretty boring without the unexpected and the unpredictable—the off-the-wall customer or vendor, the production deadline almost missed, the power outage that crashes the computers just before the print run. Something to groan or laugh about later and share with friends and family on the weekend. But if you step back, you will see that what is happening now is of an entirely new dimension.

It's not just the increase in the rate of business change—we all know markets are moving faster. It's that the magnitude of the increase is making the future completely unpredictable. It's not just that customers know more and want more; we all know that the nature of our relationship with them is changing. It's that their needs and demands are no longer predictable. It's not just that competition has heated up—we all know the basic rules of competition have been rewritten by deregulation, the breakdown of industry boundaries, globalization, and nonstop technological shifts. It's that we can no longer predict which rules will change next. We are experiencing what scholars call discontinuities, drastic changes that destroy companies, reinvent industries, and make skills obsolete. Discontinuities, coupled with an accelerating pace of change, make a mockery of the very notion of long-range planning.

> **Sooner or later, something fundamental in your business world will change.**
>
> —Andrew S. Grove, chairman and CEO, Intel Corporation, and author, *Only the Paranoid Survive*

At the beginning of this decade, senior managers at Mazda Motor Corporation looked around their world and planned for their company's future. The Japanese economy was thriving, and the public was clamoring for luxury cars. Everyone was sure the good times were going to keep rolling, so Hiroshima-based Mazda, the smallest of Japan's large car makers with sales of more than $2.5 billion in the first half of 1997, spent $550 million erecting its Hofu assembly plant to manufacture upscale cars. The plant, which was a marvel of automated manufacturing and worker-friendly industrial design, opened in 1992. In 1996 it was running at only 35 percent of capacity. What happened? Japan had entered an economic slump. Public fancy had abruptly turned from sedans and toward trucks and vans.

In another time, Mazda's predictions and plans might have worked out just fine. In another time, we might have considered the sudden changes that led to the company's mishap as nothing more than anomalies on the business radar screen, rare exceptions to the common experience. Not now. Not in the climate of uncertainty and unpredictability that is rapidly overtaking us all. When the future can no longer be counted on, the best-laid plans, based on the most elaborate and ingenious research, are doomed to fail.

> When faced with a new competitive threat—a discontinuous innovation, something that breaks with the status quo—the tendency in most organizations is to get really good at doing what they've always done. Unfortunately, while that may provide some temporary salvation, in the long run it is a dead end.
>
> —JAMES M. UTTERBACK,
> *MASTERING THE DYNAMICS OF*
> *INNOVATION*

In recent years we have witnessed an accumulation of discontinuities, like meteor showers across the business firmament, and every sign indicates they are going to continue and multiply. We are confronting an entirely new business landscape where our traditional assumptions and practices are no longer valid. Our very existence as businesses, even industries, is threatened. If we are to survive and thrive, we must find new ways to think about these discontinuities, new ways to organize our enterprises to exploit them, and new ways to turn them to extraordinary advantage.

Corporate Kinetics is our answer. We believe that the insights contained in this book will allow businesses to weather the storm of unpredictability. More than that, we believe this book will help businesses seize the opportunities inherent in an unpredictable future as they constantly create new sources of competitive advantage.

Our proposals aren't simply theory. They have emerged in part from our study of dozens of leading companies that have recognized the sea change in the business environment and have developed new ways to cope with it. We have also explored successful small and midsize companies that have demonstrated the flexibility and adaptive skills the death of predictability demands. In the pages that follow, we show how organizations such as Microsoft Corporation, Kinko's, Inc., and even the United States Army are following some of the paths we espouse.

Most of all, though, we offer a model of what we call the *kinetic enterprise,* a guide to the design of a business that can cope with the new reality. It is based on a simple yet profound insight: If we can no longer depend on our ability to predict the future, we must create a dynamic business design that can capitalize on the unpredictable, to turn it to our advantage.

The word *kinetic* derives from the Greek *kinesis,* which means movement. In physics, any body in motion—a molecule of water heated to boiling, a hammer striking an anvil, a rocket blasting off—possesses kinetic energy. In the same way, a kinetic enterprise moves, instantly responding to new demands and seizing new opportunities, adapting and evolving with every tick of the clock.

It is very different, in structure and behavior, from the traditional corporation as we know it. The kinetic enterprise isn't constrained by existing work processes. It is an instant-action machine, constantly changing its work and evolving its operations to address the unpredictable. What is more, it ignores traditional hierarchies and boundaries. Workers initiate and manage its activities, collaborating with one another at every level and within every area. The old command-and-control management model is defunct. Instead, a new culture motivates workers to collaborate spontaneously, make decisions, take risks, innovate, and learn.

> **The organization that is successful is the one that can best deal with surprise.**
>
> —GENERAL GORDON R.
> SULLIVAN AND MICHAEL V.
> HARPER, *HOPE IS NOT
> A METHOD*

The kinetic enterprise is organized around workers who initiate and execute individual, discrete, and unpredictable projects that we call *events*. Events come in two basic varieties: *market events,* which seize unpredictable market opportunities, and *customer events,* which satisfy unpredictable customer demands.

Both customer and market events require workers who are committed to the success of the overall enterprise, rather than just their own position, department, or team. Workers are expected to play a new role, initiating events and piloting them through to their conclusion. To execute events, each worker must tap the full range of human and other resources within the enterprise. They must develop the broader skills of organization, communication, and innovation in addition to their particular expertise, be it as a customer service representative, a purchasing agent, or even a lathe operator.

An event unfolds altogether; its various facets develop simultaneously. For workers to preside over these events, to work together as a team, to spur the enterprise into instant action, they require communications and information technology that lets each worker know what the organization knows, monitor operations in real time, and communicate with anyone, anytime, anywhere.

Let's take a look at some real-life examples of market and customer events.

MARKET EVENTS

A market event begins when a market opportunity is identified by a worker or team of workers and ends with the introduction of a totally new kind of product or service.

At Kinko's, for example, a copy-machine operator had a brainstorm. Kinko's is based in Ventura, California, and has some 800 locations in seven countries. During the month of December, however, customers spent more time shopping for gifts than they spent making copies or preparing presentations. The operator's idea was to use the store's new color copy technology and its laminating and binding equipment to produce gift calendars using the customer's own photographs. This worker perfected and promoted the idea within his store and then tried it out. It became an instant hit. Customers walked in with twelve of their own favorite photographs and walked out with a unique personalized holiday gift. The operator explained his idea in a phone message to Kinko's founder and chairperson, Paul Orfalea, who rushed it to the company's management and store managers via the voice mail network. Today, custom calendars are moneymakers worldwide.

At MTV Networks, a New York–based subsidiary of Viacom Inc., a market event started with a memo dubbed the Melissa Manifesto. "Screw the maudlin death images. . . . We want a cleaner, brighter, more fun MTV," proclaimed the critique written by two twenty-five-year-old production assistants, both named Melissa. The memo eventually landed on the desks of Tom Freston, CEO of MTV Networks, and Judy McGrath, president of MTV. They loved it. McGrath even jokingly told a colleague, "I feel like blowing everybody out and putting these people in charge." The Melissa Manifesto sparked a network-wide overhaul that included fresh programming, remodeled studios that overlooked Times Square, and new on-air personalities.

At Minnesota Mining and Manufacturing (3M) in St. Paul, Minnesota, a market event began when William McKnight, then CEO, broke his leg and had to wear a heavy, cumbersome plaster cast. He challenged his scientists to come up with something more comfortable, and they obliged. They took a synthetic material that was stronger and lighter than plaster and designed a process to manufacture the first fiberglass-reinforced synthetic casting tape. It takes plaster-soaked cloth casts up to a day to harden, but the new material took just minutes. The market event ended with the introduction of Scotchcast Casting Tape in the marketplace, where it became the standard material for orthopedic casts.

Market events let workers see and seize embryonic opportunities the instant they appear. The kinetic enterprise is designed to allow and encourage the entire organization to ignite market events. All the resources of the enterprise are poised to be mobilized instantly by workers.

CUSTOMER EVENTS

With sales topping $11 billion annually, Deere & Co., based in Moline, Illinois, is the world's largest manufacturer of farm equipment. It is also a leading producer of industrial and lawn equipment. At Deere, customer events are a fixture. A recent one began when a farmer decided to grow a new hybrid corn that had to be planted in tight rows. The farmer went to his local Deere dealership and explained his problem to a salesman, who rattled off a series of questions: How far apart should the seeds be dropped? How many rows must be planted? How much and what type of fertilizer must be added at the time of planting? How will the furrow be opened and closed, and to what kind of tractor will the planter be attached? An order was generated and electronically transmitted to a Deere factory. In less than sixteen hours a factory team created a one-of-a-kind planter, which was then shipped to the farmer.

The event ended when the farmer received his customized planter.

At Sumitomo Forestry Co., Ltd., a subsidiary of the Tokyo-based Sumitomo Group, a customer event starts in cyberspace. There, salespeople assist customers in designing their dream house on the screen—basement to rooftop—drawing on the nearly limitless options in the system's database. Once decisions have been made, a complete list of the necessary materials is instantly delivered along with the total bill. Simultaneously, the computer generates an order form and assigns the project to a construction team that will quickly build the house. The event ends when the construction is completed.

A customer event at New York–based Merrill Lynch & Co., Inc., began when managers at a large chemicals company asked to alter the company's relationship. Would Merrill Lynch, with sales of more than $22 billion a year, take on administration of the company's employee benefits program? It represented an emerging field for Merrill, but the opportunity was too big to ignore. Merrill created an employee benefits administration function. In the course of the customer event, Merrill added a new technology infrastructure, including automated voice response, document imaging systems, and sophisticated workstation technology with graphical user interface and connectivity to underlying systems. The customer event ended when Merrill Lynch introduced the new service to a single customer.

Customer events unleash workers to satisfy unique customer requirements. All the resources of the kinetic enterprise are poised for mobilization the moment they're needed.

THE CASE FOR KINETICS

In today's world, companies are pursuing a predictable future, a future that no longer exists. Companies rise and fall on their ability to predict. Their actions typically take the form of periodic death-defying leaps from one market to the next, one product to the next, one organizational model to the next. The kinetic business grows and evolves spontaneously with each and every market and customer event. Kinetic capabilities enable businesses to create one-of-a-kind products and services for single customers or to exploit new market opportunities, and do it profitably and pronto. When the unexpected occurs, the enterprise handles it on the fly, instantly innovating. As a result, it is constantly creating discontinuities for its competitors.

In the world of unpredictability, you're either kinetic or you're dead. Christine Albertini, a vice president and general manager for Steelcase Inc., the world's largest office furniture manufacturer based in Grand Rapids, Michigan, put it in these terms: "You need to be out of control. You have to come to peace with this. Predictability, order, control—they are not the end-all, be-all." In fact, simply recognizing the arrival of the new order, the steady diet of unpredictability, is a tough assignment.

Back in 1996 the leaders of the world's auto manufacturers could congratulate themselves on at least one area of their industry that was free of turmoil: their relationships with dealers, which had been stable for decades. But that year a shadow named H. Wayne Huizenga crossed their path, and he has not gone away.

Auto manufacturers have traditionally kept close control over the prices they charge and the numbers and varieties of models they allot to dealers. Then on the horizon appeared Huizenga, sports mogul (he owns football's Miami Dolphins, baseball's Florida Marlins, and hockey's Florida Panthers) and now chairman and co-chief executive of Republic Industries, a conglomerate in Fort Lauderdale, Florida, with sales of some $3 billion in 1997. Huizenga, who at one time drove a garbage truck for a living, had built two *Fortune* 500 companies, Waste Management (now WMX Technologies, Inc.) and Blockbuster Entertainment (purchased by Viacom in 1994). True to his record with Waste Management (where he consolidated hundreds of mom-and-pop outfits into a disposal-industry powerhouse) and Blockbuster (where he showed the video industry how to break through old decentralized retail patterns), he created a new model for selling cars. Through his fledgling automobile venture, AutoNation USA, he purchased more than one hundred car outlets selling more than thirty brands. He has also set up eleven automobile superstores and taken over three major car-rental companies (Alamo Rent-a-Car, National Car Rental Systems, and Value Rent-a-Car). And then he proceeded to sell most or all of these brands from each dealership—a total departure from the past. By the year 2000, Republic could have eighty to ninety AutoNation superstores, 200 to 250 new-car dealerships in the fifty top U.S. markets, and sales of up to $20 billion annually. That's more than The Coca-Cola Company, Intel Corporation, and Xerox Corporation generate today.

Clearly, no automaker can ignore a man who can move such quantities of cars—whether he's demanding more than his share of the most popular models or a better price. The auto manufacturers have taken notice. They never imagined, and their experts never predicted, that someone like Huizenga, who had formerly rewritten the rules of the waste-disposal and video-rental industries, would redefine the automotive market-place.

Companies must abandon their old ways and prepare to operate in the unpredictable world. They must design organizations that are ready for anything. For example:

• In the predictable world, an intelligent, seasoned super-market buyer would study population trends, which show an impending change in the ethnic makeup of his company's cus-tomer base. He would develop plans to prepare for this demo-graphic shift, such as locking in long-term contracts for delivery of the fruits and vegetables that the new majority fancies. He would move quickly, of course, because his competitors are also intelligent and seasoned, and they, too, can forecast population trends.

In the unpredictable world, a company must be ready for anything. If a new kind of food store, a sort of roving grocery-on-wheels, captures a major share of the market or a competitor latches onto a new hydroponics technology and starts to grow exotic fruits and vegetables in a warehouse next door, the buyer and his supermarket are in trouble.

• In the predictable world, an account executive at an advertising agency might see the Internet's potential as a dynamic new channel for distributing her clients' messages. She would put together a team of cyberliterate designers, writers, and artists. She would then assign her promotion group to develop an in-person and online presentation to demonstrate the agency's growing online capabilities.

In the unpredictable world, Microsoft creates its own advertising agency, which it staffs with the absolute best talent and supports with endless online promotion. The Federal Communications Commission (FCC) clamps down on the profusion of ads cluttering the World Wide Web. Surveys show that the public is more resistant to online advertising than any other form. The account executive and her ad agency are in trouble.

In the unpredictable world, these kinds of discontinuities are redefining whole industries and rendering companies obsolete. They are denying managers the sense of security that they once took as their birthright. It used to be easy to predict the future: Map industry trends, plot customer needs, scout new technologies, and plumb spreadsheets. Now all bets are off. Managers are forever off balance, vainly striving to make outmoded strategies, systems, and hierarchies match new realities.

Lawrence A. Bossidy, the respected chairman and CEO of AlliedSignal Inc., the $13-billion-a-year defense and auto parts giant based in Morristown, New Jersey, and formerly the number two man at General Electric Company in Fairfield, Connecticut, offered his view of the problem in a *Fortune* magazine interview:

> I don't think the strategic plan of yesterday has anything to do with the strategic plan of tomorrow. I can remember, in times past, working on books that were at least six inches thick. We would have a long session and take those books, put them back on the shelf, and say, "Well, that's it for another year." I want our people to understand that what you did in a strategic plan yesterday can be appropriately discarded tomorrow and with no shame and no blame, but rather a recognition that the marketplace has changed and therefore we have to change.

Similarly, Robert B. Shapiro, chairman, president, and chief executive officer of Monsanto Company, the St. Louis, Missouri, pharmaceutical and chemicals giant, says, "According to a *Harvard Business Review* article, forecasting usually meant extrapolating recent trends. So we almost never predicted the critical discontinuities in which the real money was made and lost—the changes that really determined the future of the business."

It's irreversible, and it is going to get worse, for reasons that become more and more evident: Old strategies are beat. Old boundaries are gone. Old customer loyalties are dead. Old pace is outpaced. The world has shrunk.

OLD STRATEGIES ARE BEAT

Companies no longer survive and grow by winning a share of today's markets. Sellers win by rewriting the rules of their business, making competitors' strategies a moot point. Starbucks Corporation, based in Seattle, Washington, rewrote the rules for coffeehouses; Barnes & Noble, Inc., based in New York, turned bookstores into cafes and social centers; and Amazon.com, also in Seattle, Washington, went beyond physical bookstores to provide instant book sales and delivery via the Internet. San Francisco, California's Wells Fargo & Company, came up with grocery stores that substitute for bank branches, and HomeRuns (Boston, Massachusetts), Peapod Inc. (Skokie, Illinois), and Pink Dot Inc. (Malibu, California) provided a substitute for the grocery store with online shopping and home delivery. Hospitals offer treatments that replace six-week hospital stays with four one-hour outpatient visits. The Walt Disney Company, the Burbank, California–based entertainment giant with sales of more than $11 billion a year, is creating new standards for health care communities.

OLD BOUNDARIES ARE GONE

On the Internet every day more books are sold than at Barnes & Noble's three largest stores, more music CDs than at New York's Tower Records, more cars than at Los Angeles's largest car dealership. And it's not just in cyberspace that newcomers are invading a variety of once-sacrosanct markets.

Bankers sell insurance, and insurers operate managed care

networks of hospitals, physicians, and other specialists. General Motors is in the credit card business. H. J. Heinz Company runs weight loss clinics. Circuit City Stores, Inc., sells used cars; Sara Lee Corporation, bras (in fact, one every fifteen seconds); and The Limited, Inc., CDs. Hewlett-Packard Company is even challenging giants Eastman Kodak Company and Polaroid Corporation in the camera business.

Governments are drastically loosening regulatory reins on finance, electric power, telephones, and more. As a consequence, entire companies, even entire industries, are remaking themselves. In the United States, two electric utilities, UtiliCorp United Inc. (Kansas City, Missouri) and PECO Energy Company (Philadelphia, Pennsylvania), are joining forces with a phone company (AT&T Corporation) and a provider of security-alarm services (ADT, Ltd.) to do what has never been done before: allow consumers to purchase their natural gas, electric, phone, Internet, and home security service from a single service organization.

Old Customer Loyalties Are Dead

Television, telephones, computers, the Internet, and mail order (in short, the communications revolution) have given consumers access to the full range of the world's products and services on their own terms. Gradually, overwhelmingly, consumers are deserting their old standby companies and are turning comparison shopping into a permanent art form. Their unpredictable demands for products and services tailored to their individual needs are forcing a retail transformation.

In 1997, audience share for the three major U.S. television networks dropped below 50 percent for the first time. And similar statistics hold true for businesses of all types. It used to be that only Kellogg's Corn Flakes would do; now a cheaper flake is a better flake. It used to be that only FedEx would do; now overnight is overnight.

In retailing, category-killers like Union, New Jersey–based Bed Bath & Beyond, Inc., Richmond, Virginia–based Circuit City Stores, Inc., Dallas-based CompUSA, Inc., and Atlanta-based The Home Depot, Inc., sent customer expectations soaring. We bought our cars at the nearby used-car dealer that carried about 75 autos until we went to Circuit City's CarMax, which carries 500 cars. We bought our books at the local bookstore with 20,000 titles until we shopped at a Barnes & Noble superstore with more than 150,000 titles. We bought our pet supplies at the little neighborhood pet store that carried 3,000 items until Phoenix, Arizona–based PETsMART, Inc., moved in with 12,000 items in stock.

What's the problem?

Whatever a customer wants today may not be what he or she wants tomorrow. Or he or she may want more of it. If you're offering low prices, customers want those prices slashed further. If you're offering speed or service, they want it faster or better. If you're offering state-of-the-art products, they want them newer still. In meeting ever-increasing customer demands for lower, faster, better, and newer, companies are driving themselves and their competitors to the brink.

Old Pace Is Outpaced

We all know that the pace of life has quickened over the last decade or two. A simple statistic: The average U.S. employee now works the equivalent of an extra month per year compared to his or her counterpart in 1970. The pace of business has gone into overdrive.

Take product development as an example. In 1981, 2,700 new products hit grocery shelves. By 1996 that number had swelled to nearly 20,000—a new product every half hour. New Brunswick, New Jersey–based Johnson & Johnson alone introduced nearly 300 new products worldwide in 1996; Wooster, Ohio–headquartered Rubbermaid Inc., almost one a day; Tokyo, Japan–based Sony Corporation, four a week. An automaker used to take six years to develop a new car and present it with great bravado; today the bravado is still there, but it celebrates a new car every two years.

Not only new products but endless variations on old ones are crowding the shelves and showrooms. 3M's famous little yellow Post-it Notes now come in eighteen colors, twenty-seven sizes, fifty-six standard shapes, and twenty fragrances. San Francisco–based Levi Strauss & Co. makes an incredible sixty-five thousand distinct combinations of brand, color, design, fabric, and size.

New manufacturing technologies allow companies to turn out products faster, cheaper, and in greater variety than ever before. For example, Lucent Technologies, Inc., formerly Bell Laboratories, has opened a factory in New Jersey that assembles wireless handsets in just four minutes. In Greensboro, North Carolina, AMP Inc., a leading manufacturer of electronic connectors, among other products, produces parts for automotive antilock braking systems in twelve to sixteen seconds.

> Because business life cycles are now measured in months rather than years, executives must plan for their new products' replacement at almost the same time that they launch them.
>
> —MICHAEL L. TUSHMAN,
> COLUMBIA UNIVERSITY
> MANAGEMENT PROFESSOR,
> *JOURNAL OF BUSINESS STRATEGY*

THE WORLD HAS SHRUNK

In 1990, Dean LeBaron, founder of Batterymarch Financial Management, based in Boston, and a pioneer in emerging market investing, flew from the United States to the then Soviet Union, an enigmatic country whose rivalry with his own had shaped the course of so much history in the past half-century. The Soviet Union had been for him an inexplicably malevolent place, as it had been for most Americans of his generation (he was fifty-seven at the time). Yet there he was, the consummate capitalist, on his way to pursue business in the Soviet Union. And, he told himself, if reforms work, Western businessmen and -women would follow in droves.

He was right—and not only about Russia.

"Business isn't going global," LeBaron observed during a 1997 fact-finding trip to China. "It's gone global." These days, Silicon Valley competes with Silicon Bog (in Ireland), Silicon Jungles (in India and Singapore), Silicon Glen (in Scotland), and Silicon Forest (in Germany and Switzerland). Half of the globe's software code is written in third world nations, the lion's share in India. Redwood City, California–based VeriFone, Inc. publishes its "Letter from the Chairman" in seven languages; Ford's 371,702 employees speak more than fifty different languages and dialects and work in manufacturing facilities in thirty countries on six continents.

The world's fastest growing markets lie outside the United States. More than half of the revenues reported by U.S. giants Coca-Cola, Intel, McDonald's Corporation, and The Procter & Gamble Company now come from foreign countries.

These signs of seismic change in the United States and around the world are more than straws in the wind. They show that the current era of unpredictability has its roots deep within our organizations and our culture, and that it is here to stay. It will get worse before—and if—it gets better.

Many managers, recognizing the need to do something, are revamping their companies. Unfortunately, they often base their change on yet another market prediction or yet another apparent trend-in-the-making. They seek to ratchet up their product development speed or drastically trim their staff to cut costs and push decision-making closer to the front line. From time to time these companies actually realize some short-term gains, although when the Society of Human Resource Management surveyed 1,468 downsized companies, it found that productivity had stayed the same or declined in more than half of them. The problem: They failed to alter their basic business philosophy and practice. You can't expect to cope with revolutionary change by making minor adjustments in a current, static, business design.

> **When an organization is experiencing disruption by internal or external forces, it can either try to hold on to stability, and lose its ability to adapt and survive, or it can respond in a dynamic manner.**
>
> —CAROL KINSEY GOMAN,
> COMMUNICATION WORLD

THE KINETIC WAY

We believe that kinetics meets the dire need for a new business model that can cope profitably with unceasing surprise and discontinuity. The kinetic model allows companies in all industries and of all sizes to accommodate customers' disparate, unexpected needs. It enables them to mobilize instantly to exploit evanescent market opportunities.

Here's how: In the kinetic enterprise, hierarchy is dead. Workers operate like nodes on an enterprise-wide network. There are no rigid organization charts or job descriptions that specify what workers will do day after day. Instead, they are wired to customers, to each other, to suppliers, and to outside experts. Frontline workers, discovering an unexpected market opportunity or spotting an unpredictable customer need, marshal the resources they need to get the job done. They may tap workers at all levels of the organization, inside and outside the enterprise. Because everyone else in the enterprise also thinks and acts like a frontline worker, they immediately respond. Virtual teams constantly form and dissolve to get the job done. Computer systems, factories, and service operations are specifically designed to allow this interaction. Together, the spontaneous team decides what it will produce and how it will do it.

The kinetic enterprise is not just a pipe dream. Companies such as Buckman Laboratories International, Chevron Corporation, Coca-Cola, Dell Computer Corporation, Hewlett-Packard, Albert Einstein Healthcare Network, Intel, Kaiser Permanente, Kinko's, Lands' End, Microsoft, MCI Communications Corporation, MTV Networks, Oticon, The Charles Schwab Corporation, Sears, Roebuck and Co., Southwest Airlines Co., Thermo Electron Corporation, Visa International, and USAA are progressing along the path toward becoming kinetic. So is—surprise!—the United States Army.

Over the last two decades the Army has been battered by unexpected and unpredictable change, from the sudden end of the cold war to the launching of Desert Storm, from peacekeeping missions in Macedonia and the Sinai to the delivery of humanitarian assistance in Bosnia, Rwanda, and Somalia.

In their book *Hope Is Not a Method,* former Army Chief of Staff Gordon R. Sullivan and Michael V. Harper describe the

Army's response to this drum roll of surprises—the creation of a flexible, versatile, kinetic organization. By making major changes in its traditional command-and-control management system, they say, "when the time came we could tailor a response and get it about right."

The new Army, called Force XXI, is a smaller, adaptable force that can immediately plan and engage in new kinds of missions. To respond to unexpected and diverse missions, the new Army is prepared to move forces quickly to virtually any region of the globe and to respond with great flexibility. Force XXI is capable of learning and adapting even while conducting operations. Information is the new source of power: Major technology initiatives are beginning to give soldiers far more information about where they are—and where the enemy is—than any fighting force in history. In the not so distant future, every platoon and tank crew will have real-time information on what's going on around them, the location of the enemy, and the nature and targeting of the enemy's weapons system. Armed with this information, soldiers will function as their own commanders, making decisions on the fly.

The handiwork of Sullivan and other generals made the headlines, but the real news was in the doing—in the practices that inspired soldiers to march to their own drummer.

Change has also become the hallmark of another behemoth, this one in the world of retailing. In 1992, Sears Roebuck went through one revolution, led by chairman and chief executive officer Arthur C. Martinez. The company cut costs, did away with the catalog, and repositioned the stores to emphasize its "softer side." Profits jumped, and Sears stock more than tripled in value.

But Martinez has absorbed the kinetic message: Even the most successful of organizations cannot afford to rest on their laurels in a world gone unpredictable. He has started a second revolution. The company's real strength for the future, Martinez says, is in its brands, such as Craftsman and Kenmore, and Sears is establishing thousands of small stores to sell those brands. Only 22 of the 380 new operations Sears opened in 1997 were big stores; the rest were the new freestanding brand-name units.

The old-time retailer has been able to change direction twice within just a handful of years. In his 1996 letter to share-holders, Martinez explained one reason that has been possible: "Transformation requires a work force, from top to bottom, that is committed to embracing and fostering change. . . . Associates must think like owners if we are to keep the process of continuous reinvention alive inside the company."

One Sears innovation, so-called learning maps, depict the essential business conditions that all employees need to grasp how what they do each day contributes to store results and overall competitiveness. The "Sears Money Map," for example, is a Monopoly-like game in which employees place bets on the sources and uses of funds as they flow from the customer's wallet to the bottom line. Employees, on average, believe Sears makes 45 cents per dollar of sales. The real number is 1.5 cents. When employees understand their company, their place in it, and their responsibility in the scheme of things, and when they are properly motivated and rewarded, they make the enter-prise hum.

Martinez made the headlines, but the real news was in the doing—in the training and inspiration that enabled workers to turn a retailing supertanker on a dime . . . again and again.

> It's all about time. The future is now. Not the next five years but the next five minutes.
>
> —ROB RODIN, PRESIDENT AND
> CEO, MARSHALL INDUSTRIES,
> FAST COMPANY

In this chapter we argued that predictability is dead. It is now manifest that the business world's future is unpredictable, unknowable, chaotic.

To survive and flourish, companies must turn chaos to their advantage. We have suggested some of the ways in which kinet-ics makes that possible, and in the pages that follow we will describe just how it works and how you can prepare to apply it.

We will show how workers on every level act as opportunity champions, recognizing market opportunities that no manage-ment team could ever see and pursuing these opportunities to a successful conclusion. We will discuss the role of customer advocates in riding herd on customer events, marshaling the skills and experience of dozens of different workers to respond to unexpected customer demands. We will suggest how to put into place the business model and technological tools essential to the successful operation of a kinetic enterprise.

Some of the world's pioneering companies have already begun the long, necessary march toward a kinetic reality. We will describe their efforts and experiences. But we urge you now, as you read these words, to start thinking about how you can apply the kinetic approach to your own business. Think big and learn fast. Time is running out.

CHAPTER 2

THINK THE UNPREDICTABLE

SEIZE UNEXPECTED MARKET OPPORTUNITIES

> **At the heart of kinetics is a radical new way to compete. A kinetic business capitalizes on the unexpected. It immediately and profitably exploits new opportunities.**

ABOUT 1990, Intel, the world's top maker of integrated circuits with sales of more than $20 billion in 1996, was just beginning to have some major successes with its microprocessor. It was also developing the next-generation chip that would become known far and wide as the Pentium. The fly in the ointment was the technical backwardness of that day's computers, particularly what is known as the bus—the circuitry, wires, and other hardware that transmit data within a computer and across a network. At the time, the bus simply couldn't handle data as fast as the Pentium could dish it up.

Then a group of Intel scientists came up with an idea. Why not create a new and faster bus and make it part of Intel's product line? After all, it fit perfectly with Intel's *strategic purpose*—to be the "building-block supplier to the computing industry worldwide." The scientists also had a clear notion of just how to design such a bus. But the project would take a major infusion of cash, and that meant selling the idea to top management—in particular, to Andrew S. Grove, the company's CEO and guiding genius.

Grove turned the scientists down flat. Mainframe manufacturers like International Business Machines (IBM) had always produced buses, and Grove thought Intel should not poach on its customers' preserve. In the end, though, thanks to a culture that promoted persistence, the scientists prevailed. They convinced Grove that the new bus would be a boon to the whole industry and that Intel should manufacture it.

A year later, at an industry meeting, Grove stood on a stage to demonstrate how Intel's bus, plus its new chip, made it possible for a personal computer to get e-mail over a wireless network. The achievement was hailed by all major computer manufacturers, and their representatives stood with Grove onstage.

Overnight, it seemed, Intel had emerged as a leader in bus design and production, adding to its aura of invincibility. And it all happened because a team of workers was looking for an unpredictable market opportunity, found one, and convinced the boss that they knew better than he where the company should be headed. It all happened because Intel exhibits the characteristics of a kinetic corporation.

Kinetic enterprises prepare for the unpredictable future by enabling inventive workers—which means anyone from receptionist to chief executive—to act as opportunity champions, turning their ideas into new products, new services, and even new businesses. In fact, kinetic workers effectively invent their companies' futures, forcing competitors to play catch-up or perish.

Traditionally, companies have sought advantage with strategies that required death-defying leaps from one competency to the next, one generation of products to the next, one market to the next, even one business to the next. Kinetic enterprises still invest in big market plays, but they also enable workers to exploit opportunities that leaders can't see. This results in thousands of smaller ideas created and piloted to completion by well-rewarded, fired-up workers. We have labeled them *market events*.

We define a market event as *the work of the enterprise immediately and profitably performed to seize an unexpected market opportunity*. In a market event, the work of the enterprise encompasses everything needed to bring a new idea to market:

- It starts when a worker or workers (in Intel's case, a team of scientists) scan the horizon for an unpredictable opportunity and find one (the need for a new bus).

- It continues as the worker or workers assess the opportunity's impact on the enterprise (the cost to design and manufacture a new bus) and determine whether that impact is desirable (expected sales for the new bus and bus-enabled chip). That answer will also depend on how closely the impact hews to the business's strategic purpose (at Intel, a match).

- If the worker or workers decide to go ahead, the next step is to marshal the resources of the enterprise to capitalize on the opportunity (get the budget go-ahead) and proceed to develop and implement the best approach to the task (how Intel will manufacture and market the new bus).

• The market event ends when the worker or workers roll out the innovation to the enterprise (the bus goes into production).

WHAT MARKET EVENTS AREN'T

Market events aren't strategy. In a kinetic enterprise, leadership teams still set strategic objectives. Leaders know, however, that workers must innovate in unexpected directions as unpredictable shifts occur. Therefore, leaders also prepare organizations for market events. Leaders create a new kind of vision—one that describes outrageous customer benefits. Using this vision, the leaders set boundaries to determine which market opportunities the organization will or will not respond to.

Market events aren't market forecasting. Leading-edge companies have recognized that markets are fragmenting at an accelerating pace. To win the innovation game, companies are designing new products and services for smaller and smaller markets. In kinetic enterprises, marketing professionals still monitor and respond to visible trends, doing their best to forecast market size and product life, but when something unexpected occurs, they don't wait for next year's planning. They exploit the unexpected by launching their own market event.

This doesn't mean, however, that with every market event, workers are predicting the next new market. By spotting embryonic opportunities visible only on the firing line, workers invent and offer something brand new to one or a handful of customers. When a new idea succeeds, it is captured by the company's knowledge bank, ready for workers across the enterprise to apply.

Market events aren't just responses to shifting customer needs. Not every unexpected market opportunity emerges from shifting customer needs.

Breakthroughs in new technology (such as the Internet or genetic correction of health problems), radical new business designs (such as build-to-order manufacturing), or government regulatory decisions can radically impact a company's current and future business. These unexpected opportunities—or, more commonly, their unexpected timing—allow workers to invent ahead of customer needs. Workers update internal processes, invent new products and services, and design new businesses to deliver benefits that customers have never received or imagined. In the process, these market events may create industry discontinuities that force competitors to change or perish.

At most companies these days, innovation occurs quite differently: Executives and marketers monitor economic, regulatory, demographic, and competitive trends. Then they predict future opportunities and select those to be pursued by product managers. Meanwhile, researchers focus on promising new technologies. For example, R&D groups at many automobile manufacturers are working to develop affordable and practical electric cars.

The problem: Many of the market shifts and discontinuities that reshape an industry's future do not appear on the radar screen of this select group of executives, marketers, product developers, and researchers. In their best-selling book *Competing for the Future,* management theorists Gary Hamel and C. K. Prahalad argue that "seeing the future first may be more about having a wide-angle lens than a crystal ball." To create that wide-angle lens, they recommend establishing an executive-led special-projects team to investigate industry discontinuities once a year or so.

We take an entirely different approach. In a kinetic enterprise, workers are the wide-angle lens. A kinetic worker can be anyone—sales and customer service representatives, men and women on the assembly line, information technology specialists, or international managers. By initiating and participating in market events—that is, actively working to understand the marketplace, constantly watching for the unexpected, and piloting new products and services—kinetic workers gain a deep understanding of brand-new customers, brand-new technologies, and brand-new product and service concepts. They develop certainty about timing, about what is real and what is not, and about what works and what doesn't.

The manufacturing team that pilots single- and small-lot manufacturing techniques has far better insight into the impact on operations of new custom-made products than any vice president of marketing. The surgeon who spots and pilots a new kind of robotic surgical technology has far better insight into the future of remote surgery than any boardroom executive. The customer service representative who takes orders and listens to customer complaints all day has far better insight into product weaknesses than the product's sales manager.

A market event is sometimes a watershed in a company's history, an idea or innovation that suddenly moves the organization into a brand-new market or inspires a merger. But the real power of kinetics is evolutionary, not revolutionary.

Just as the company's ability to meet unpredictable customer demands develops with each customer event, so the company's ability to capitalize on unexpected market opportunities grows with each market event. Both kinds of events typically consist of a small, incremental effort whose outcome is reported throughout the organization. That way, workers in different locations can learn about the new insight or innovation and find different ways to apply it. The learning process is continual, as is the steady buildup of organizational know-how. This is how the kinetic enterprise evolves in step with emerging, fragmenting, shifting markets—one customer, one idea, one product, one service, one event at a time.

In this chapter, we describe a range of market events. First, though, we offer a scenario of how these market events might play out at an enterprise of our own imagining. We call it Global Media, Inc.

THE CASE OF GLOBAL MEDIA, INC.

The days when telecommunications, cable television, software, personal computers, entertainment, and publishing existed as separate industries have long since passed. A handful of media conglomerates, Global Media among them, have emerged from the confusion.

Global Media's senior management doesn't try to dictate the production or delivery of specific products or services, or the maintenance of relationships with specific customers. They all change too fast. A new generation of technology arrives every six months, competitive products or services appear every six minutes, and customers can switch to a competitor in six seconds. If Global Media does not continuously innovate and evolve, redefining and reinventing the very nature of its business, it will die.

Global Media succeeds because its strategic purpose—"create the ultimate media lifestyle, work style, and play style for customers"—keeps its workers' adrenaline pumping at a creative high. This purpose, embraced by every worker, points them in the right direction.

• In Chicago, a market event begins when a sales representative notices an increase in the use by several local hospitals of Global Media telecommunications systems for the home monitoring of patients. He assembles a team to create a video to demonstrate all the possible home-care uses of the system to other potential hospital clients. They are suitably impressed, and several place orders for the telecommunications system. The demonstration video is put into the company's computer databank of know-how, and an e-mail alerts the worldwide sales staff to its availability there.

• In Tokyo, a market event begins when a network designer learns of a construction consortium's plans to develop a community of so-called smart homes, where built-in systems operate appliances, monitor household security, and manage energy consumption. She convinces a Global Media executive committee to finance what she hopes will be a joint venture to create smart home offices. Her presentation to the construction consortium is a triumph, and she is invited to join its R&D team. Together, the network designer and the R&D team develop the necessary new technology, which they pilot in the community of smart homes, then deposit what they have learned into Global Media's worldwide know-how databank.

• In an Asian nation, the government deregulates the country's telecommunications industry, which allows Global Media to sell its products and services there for the first time. A market event begins when a Global Media regional manager detects a strong interest in a new kind of retail telecommunications center where Global Media products and services can be sold via interactive displays. The regional manager recruits workers from a half-dozen company sites around the world—customer service representatives, salespeople, retail store workers—as well as outside educators to help his local workers design the new store format. In less than three months this team creates a new way to sell telecommunications products and services in this Asian market.

• In Los Angeles, a market event begins when a product development team, inspired by recent technological advances, attempts to create lapel pin communicators like those featured in the old *Star Trek* television series. Team members wire their offices, homes, and jackets to test the concept. After three months they conclude the technology is still too immature for the lapel pin device, but it could be applied to the creation of a desktop no-hands, voice-activated telephone. And that is where they turn their attention.

On Monday morning, the CEO asks his computer, "What businesses are we in today?" The reply: "This week, Global Media expanded the use of its telecommunications products to the home-care market, participated in the joint invention of smart–home office technology, created a way to sell telecommunications products and services in a newly deregulated country, and investigated a technology that will allow it to develop a desktop voice-activated telephone."

Quick! What Business Are We In?

—Norwest Corporation 1996
Annual Report

What business are we in? As our eight million customers demand more convenience, as technology speeds the transmission of information, as industries evolve or evaporate, every successful company must ask itself that question.

—Richard M. Kovacevich,
chairman and CEO,
Norwest Corporation

THE ELEMENTS OF MARKET EVENTS

Although they are markedly different from one another, the market events at our imaginary company all have a common theme: Each yielded breakthroughs that were sparked by a worker's ideas and follow-through. At Global Media, workers are inspired and challenged to ignore traditional thinking and business boundaries. The company has learned a lesson that many real-life, real-time businesses must now accept: To survive in a quicksilver marketplace, an enterprise must rely on workers to innovate continually.

Now, let's examine the six basic elements of market events using our Global Media, Inc., scenario. These elements are (1) spotting an unexpected market opportunity, (2) assessing its impact on the enterprise, (3) deciding if the market opportunity is right for the business, (4) marshaling the resources of the enterprise to capitalize on the opportunity, (5) developing the best approach to the task, and (6) capturing insights and rolling out the idea to the enterprise.

In Chicago, *spotting an unexpected market opportunity,* a sales representative noticed that a few hospitals were using Global Media's telecommunications system to monitor patients in their homes. Patients would push bedside buttons to see and interact with nurses at a twenty-four-hour nursing station. Diagnostic information would be passed automatically from home to hospital. Doctors would pop in for electronic house calls and visual checks of patients.

Assessing its impact on the enterprise, the sales representative saw that increasing this new use of telecommunications would allow Global Media to expand its relationship with a dozen other hospitals in the area, thereby increasing revenues.

Deciding if the market opportunity was right for the business, the sales representative considered it in relation to the company's strategic purpose—creating the ultimate media lifestyle, work style, and play style for customers—and found that it fit perfectly.

Marshaling the resources of the enterprise to capitalize on the opportunity, the sales representative sought budget funds specifically earmarked to support workers' innovations—in this case, a video to demonstrate the uses of Global Media's technology. By sending an e-mail message to twenty-five members of the headquarters software team, the sales representative found a software developer interested in his idea. Together, they shaped the proposal, and the sales representative was awarded $10,000 by regional managers, with no questions asked by headquarters.

Developing the best approach to the task, the sales representative set up a conference call that included the software developer, a Global Media marketing expert, and a home-care specialist from a local hospital. During a two-hour call, the participants outlined a video to demonstrate the health care application. The software specialist set aside two weeks to create the demonstration video, his time and expenses paid out of the $10,000 budgeted for the project. His demonstration starred a computer-created image in the role of a nurse who reminded patients when to take their medication and prompted them with an alarm if they didn't respond. This approach, dramatizing the possibilities inherent for health care in telecommunications technology, was a hit, luring hospital executives to Global Media retail centers to review the show.

Capturing insights and rolling out the idea to the enterprise, the sales representative sent copies of the demonstration video to Global Media's international learning centers, where retail managers review innovations from other retail stores that they can apply to their markets.

In Tokyo, *spotting an unexpected market opportunity,* a Global Media network designer thought the construction of a smart-home community presented a chance for the company to get in on the ground floor of a new trend.

Assessing its impact on the enterprise, she recognized that participation in the project would require Global Media to invent new on-site technology and consumer billing, a significant investment that would have to be made by senior management.

Deciding whether the market opportunity was right for the business, the designer determined that it fit Global Media's strategic purpose.

Marshaling the resources of the enterprise to capitalize on the opportunity, she sought help via e-mail from headquarters experts in marketing, billing, and product development. They estimated the cost of creating a smart-home office system and wrote a business case for action that summarized the opportunity. The network designer then championed the idea in a conference call with funding decision-makers from sales and R&D, and they agreed to support her.

Developing and implementing the new idea, she and her virtual team worked with the construction consortium's technical people and completed the pilot in twelve weeks.

Capturing insights and rolling out the idea to the enterprise, the network designer prepared a message and sent it to sales staff worldwide: "Check the know-how databank for a new smart-home product. Smart-home architects and developers could be a big new market for us in the next few months or the next few years."

In Los Angeles, *spotting an unexpected market opportunity,* a headquarters product-development team focused on a new technology breakthrough, suggesting that the moment for replicating *Star Trek's* lapel pin telephone "communicator" might finally have arrived.

Assessing its impact on the enterprise, the team realized it would be huge, since all of Global Media's current revenues were essentially based on handheld phones.

Deciding if the market opportunity was right for the business, the team determined that its plan might not be practical, but the company would rather take a research risk than lose the chance for a breakthrough product that fit its strategic purpose.

Marshaling the resources of the enterprise to capitalize on the opportunity, the team started by securing funds. In the past, Global Media had spent millions to retool with each technology shift, but now the company sets aside a pool of funds that specifically allows its information technology professionals to research and pilot new technology. The communicator team obtained the resources to pursue its project from these funds.

Developing and implementing the new idea, the team members had their offices, homes, and jackets wired to see if they could get the device to work. They spent three months testing and redesigning the prototype. Finally, they concluded that the technology was still too immature. But they realized it could be applied to a new desktop voice-activated phone.

Capturing insights and rolling out the idea to the enterprise, the team conducted an in-person briefing for fifty technology colleagues. They reviewed their original hypothesis and the outcome of their work, they shared their insights on what was needed to make the lapel pin communicator a reality, and outlined where their attention would now be focused—on the no-hands phone.

> **If you execute, you can do anything. When a company has a clear mission, and people know how their individual mission fits into the big picture, everyone paddles in the same direction. Unfortunately, those are two of the least understood issues for most people in business: What's expected of me and how do I accomplish it? It's back to basics.**
>
> —STEPHEN COOPER, CHAIRMAN
> AND CEO, ETEC SYSTEMS, INC.,
> *FAST COMPANY*

Because our imaginary Global Media, Inc., is inevitably so technology driven, it might seem at this point that market events must have their roots in research and development. Not so. What counts is the workers' ability to recognize and seize unexpected market opportunities of any kind. Both the hospital-oriented sales representative in Chicago and the smart-home-oriented designer in Tokyo grabbed a chance to help Global Media break into a new market—and both launched a market event to see that it happened. The technological elements, for our purposes, are incidental.

STRATEGIC PURPOSE GUIDES MARKET EVENTS

In a kinetic enterprise, workers innovate on behalf of the entire enterprise wherever market events take them—but only, and always, when their ideas and the market opportunities they spot bring the company's strategic purpose to life. By understanding the strategic purpose, workers focus on market events that carry the enterprise forward. They spot market opportunities and give birth to ideas that enable the enterprise to create new products or services and evolve in unexpected, profitable ways. This purpose is a far cry from traditional corporate mission statements that are rooted in today's business environment where market share is king. Inevitably, they describe a company's particular product or business and dictate what the organization will make and sell ("We want to be the world's leading producer of VCRs").

But as our no-longer-so-stable world unwinds, as VCRs are

replaced by Web television and managers can no longer predict what will happen next, mission statements must change radically. Strategic purpose, as we call it, isn't some cute or catchy phrase coined in a moment and intended to serve as a marching song at the next office picnic. *It's a statement of the outrageous benefits promised to customers.* It states what the enterprise is striving to achieve, not what it's trying to sell.

A strategic purpose suggests benefits that customers have never received or imagined. It helps workers, who are absorbed in their immediate concerns, see the whole business picture. It frees them to innovate beyond the visible horizon and yet remain within the enterprise's strategic domain. It energizes them to accept personal responsibility for creating competitive advantages.

The single most important thing you can do to help your company thrive in the modern era of tough customers, intense competition, and relentless change is this: Help every single person in the company understand the business in the same big-picture terms that the CEO does.

—MICHAEL HAMMER,
ORIGINATOR OF
REENGINEERING
AND PRESIDENT,
HAMMER AND COMPANY,
FAST COMPANY

Microsoft's outrageous customer benefit ("information at your fingertips") isn't tied to a specific product. Rather, it's intended to leave lots of room for innovation while channeling workers' efforts toward a common goal. The outrageous benefit of automaker Toyota Motor Corporation ("anything you can do at home, you can do while in motion") serves the same end, as does technology developer Thermo Electron's ("develop technological solutions to society's problems"), Visa International's (create a universal currency), and Coca-Cola's (enable "every person on this planet to be able to choose one of our products whenever and wherever thirst strikes").

A kinetic enterprise's strategic purpose grows out of the heart and guts of the enterprise, and it typically requires months of discussion and soul-searching by all the workers. Senior managers have ultimate responsibility for establishing and communicating an enterprise's strategic purpose, but they see to it that workers, suppliers, and customers contribute directly to it.

The market event represents one kinetic solution to the dilemma posed by the unpredictable future, but there is another kind. It starts not with an inspiration from within the enterprise but with a customer's request for a special product or service. It is to this kind of event that we next turn our attention.

CHAPTER 3

DO THE UNPREDICTABLE

SATISFY UNEXPECTED CUSTOMER DEMANDS

Also at the heart of kinetics is a revolutionary way to view and serve customers. A kinetic business treats every customer interaction as discrete and unpredictable. It immediately and profitably delivers one-of-a-kind products, services, and relationships.

How will all of us—companies of every size and shape—do business in the years ahead? How will we satisfy a new generation of demanding, savvy customers who know just what they want and expect us to deliver products that fit their exact needs and desires?

The answer, we believe, is found in a collection of actions we call a customer event. It can take many forms, depending on the company and industry, but for a taste of what it's like, we suggest a visit to Dell Computer Corporation.

This is how a customer event plays out at Dell, which is based in Round Rock, Texas: A customer calls the company's 800 number and speaks with one of Dell's telephone sales representatives or logs onto its Internet site. Either way, rather than ordering one or another off-the-shelf version of a computer system—90 percent of sales are to corporations—the customer describes his or her particular needs for speed, memory, monitor size, software, and the like. The sales representative listens, asks for clarification, offers suggestions, and, together, in real time, they design the customer's ideal computer system.

Not until the customer approves the design and agrees to the price does the sales representative signal Dell's suppliers to send along the appropriate components. This careful timing enables the company to sharply reduce inventory costs. It also lets Dell take advantage of price reductions for personal computer parts and frequent improvements in technology—the parts in its machines, on average, are sixty to eighty days newer than those in an IBM or Compaq Computer Corporation computer manufactured at the same time.

Dell's production workers are trained to switch from one system design to another in the blink of an eye. An order placed at 9:00 A.M. Monday can be on a delivery truck to the customer by 9:00 P.M. Tuesday, at a price 10 to 15 percent lower than its rivals charge.

The customer's telephone or Internet connection to Dell continues after delivery. A Web site has been set up where the company's customer-support knowledge base can be accessed for a menu of solutions to individual problems.

What becomes evident in a look at Dell is its determination over the years to find new ways to meet the specific, unpredictable demands of customers—to perfect the customer event.

In a traditional organization, the work of identifying customer demands is performed largely by senior managers, who define that demand in terms of mass markets. Their "interaction" with customers is often sporadic, and once a year or so, managers predict what thousands, sometimes millions, of customers will need or want. The managers essentially design the next generation of products and services, and decide just how they will be distributed, promoted, and sold. Everything functions smoothly enough until the business runs headlong into a discontinuity. Then the managers and their companies are in deep trouble.

We define a customer event as *the work of the enterprise immediately and profitably performed to satisfy a unique, single customer demand.* In a customer event, the work of the enterprise encompasses everything needed to deliver a one-of-a-kind product, service, or relationship to a customer.

- It starts when a worker or workers (in Dell's case, a telephone sales representative) collaborates with a customer to ascertain the customer's unique and specific needs (equipment configuration, delivery and support requirements, financing terms, and future relationship needs).

- Next, the worker or workers decide if satisfying the demand is right for the business. The Dell team must determine whether or not the company can profitably make and deliver the unique computer configuration (hardware and software), service, and support needs that the customer requested.

- If the worker or workers decide to move ahead, all internal activities associated with the request are initiated. At Dell, the sales representative submits the order, which triggers the ordering of parts, assembly of the computer, shipping schedules, and billing.

• Next, the worker or workers perform the tasks necessary to fulfill the commitment and complete all related duties—assemble and ship the product, process the bill, and complete internal accounting and reporting. At Dell, the employees monitor the activities to ensure that the right computer is delivered to the customer on time.

• The customer event ends when the customer requirement is satisfied and the insights of the worker or workers are captured for future use.

WHAT CUSTOMER EVENTS AREN'T

Customer events aren't an exercise in extravagant service à la Nordstrom. You may have heard about the wheelchair-bound customer who could not find a Nordstrom shawl short enough that it would not get caught in her wheels. A few weeks later the customer received in the mail a short shawl knitted by the clerk who had waited on her.

In a kinetic enterprise, customer demands aren't satisfied because of lone heroes but because the enterprise has fundamentally rethought and redesigned its capabilities and operations to profitably deliver one-of-a-kind products and services.

Customer events aren't dedicated to achieving customer intimacy or even a long-term relationship. Customer events are precisely focused on giving customers exactly what they want, when they want it. The customer who shies away from closeness, who wants to move easily between vendors to take advantage of seasonal or occasional discounts, isn't a second-class citizen. The kinetic enterprise is designed to let the customer design his or her own sales relationship—close or otherwise.

Customer events aren't micro-marketing, aren't slicing the market finer and finer, and then producing highly tailored products and services for each segment. Each customer event is about designing and delivering a one-of-a-kind product, service, or relationship for a single customer.

Customer events aren't mass customization. Mass customization is a method of production, the capability to make tailored products based on predefined features and options. A customer event encompasses more than just production. It is all the processes of the enterprise—including selling, marketing, new product development, billing, and knowledge management—executed for a single customer.

In a kinetic enterprise, the elements of customer events happen simultaneously in an organized, continuous, well-practiced flow of ideas and actions. As workers cope with unexpected customer demands, they gain new skills and insights; these in turn become part of the company's knowledge base, where they become available to all.

Most customer events are modest in size and impact. In a kinetic enterprise, customer events enable workers, individually and as a group, to gradually become more and more skilled at helping customers get what they want. The process is evolutionary, the result of hundreds of customer events all proceeding simultaneously, continuously building the organization's expertise and flexibility.

This organic, cooperative model yields another remarkable benefit. By providing customers with unprecedented, breakthrough products, services, and relationships, the kinetic enterprise is, in effect, inventing the future—creating the unpredictable demands that its competitors will have to meet.

> **Think like the customer. Let their voices design what you do.**
>
> —ROB RODIN, PRESIDENT AND
> CEO, MARSHALL INDUSTRIES,
> *FAST COMPANY*

Now let's examine a scenario of how a customer event might play out at an enterprise of our invention. We call it Carpet, Inc.

THE CASE OF CARPET, INC.

The place is Long Beach, California, on a rainy Saturday. The time is the not so distant future. Watching a movie in her living room, Joy Nelson bolts upright as the main character walks across a canary yellow carpet. "Wow," she murmurs. "That's exactly what this room needs." She pauses the film on the television screen and dials a local carpet store, Carpet, Inc., on the built-in personal computer, Web browser, and interactive television. Instantly, a salesman's face appears on her screen.

"Canary yellow?" he asks. "And you want it installed in time for your party next week? These are the colors we have in stock." Swatches flash across the screen, but none is quite right.

"We could make something to order," the salesman suggests. "How about one of these?" A rainbow of colors, hundreds of tones, arches across the screen, allowing Nelson to examine each tint of yellow and compare it to the color of the carpet frozen in another section of her television screen. Finally, she sees exactly the shade. She aims a laser pointer at the screen and marks her choice with a tiny red light. Her selection appears on the carpet salesman's monitor.

Meanwhile, the salesman is watching a second computer-to-computer dialogue. The carpet company is scheduling production at a supplier's round-the-clock manufacturing plant that produces what seems like an endless strand of nylon fiber.

"My company is reserving a factory to produce your yellow fiber," he tells Nelson. "Would you like to order a special weight or one of our dirt-resistant or luxury textures?" After considering the options described on her screen, Nelson works out the details of her customized request with the carpet salesman. She e-mails him her floor plans, pulled from her household information archive, while he simultaneously arranges the production, pricing, and delivery of the canary carpet.

"Now," the salesman says, "may we suggest some other items to go with the carpet? I've seen some terrific pillows. Also, are you working with a decorator?"

Nelson doesn't have a decorator, but she acknowledges that

she would like to make some other changes for her party. Within seconds the carpet salesman is joined on the television screen by a decorator from one of his company's sister stores.

Nelson's video camera pans her living room. Ideas and images of throw rugs and window blinds are exchanged, selections made, prices and delivery dates reviewed.

Nelson thanks both the salesman and the decorator, and returns to her movie.

An hour later a carpet installer reviews his schedule for the coming week on a computer built into the dashboard of his truck. For his Tuesday visit with Joy Nelson, he sees the layout of her living room, a computer-generated installation plan, and a list of the special tools that have been ordered for the job. He also sees a picture of the canary carpet. He confirms the appointment, changing the time from 9:00 to 9:30 with a few strokes on his keyboard.

In Los Angeles, the carpet company's regional sales manager, watching his monitor, notices a $5,000 jump in daily revenues. In New York, a marketing manager reads an e-mail from the carpet store salesman describing the unusual order. "A yellow carpet," he muses, "and she saw it in a movie." He forwards the e-mail to a friend, an editor at a house and garden magazine, adding, "How about a piece on the newest trend in carpets? Pick a movie, pick a carpet. We started producing it the night the movie ran."

THE ELEMENTS OF CUSTOMER EVENTS

In a traditional business setting, Nelson's call might easily have ended as soon as it began. After all, she was asking for a style of carpet that the company did not make and had never made before. She was imposing an unreasonable deadline. And she had no plans to buy anything more than a yellow carpet.

But the carpet company succeeded in meeting Nelson's every need because it was designed to cope with the unpredictable, the kind of situations that arise when individual customers are allowed to design their own products, services, or relationships.

> **Imagine the capacity to do it, do it right, and do it right now. . . . Imagine the results.**
>
> —NINE WEST GROUP, 1996
> ANNUAL REPORT

Now, let's examine the six basic elements of customer events using our Carpet, Inc., scenario: (1) ascertaining a customer's specific needs, (2) assessing its impact on the enterprise, (3) deciding if satisfying the demand is right for the enterprise, (4) marshaling the resources of the enterprise to meet the customer's demand, (5) developing and implementing the best approach to the task, and (6) satisfying the customer.

Ascertaining a customer's specific needs, the carpet salesman showed Joy Nelson hundreds of color samples until she spotted one she wanted.

Assessing its impact on the enterprise, the carpet salesman determined whether the company could produce the requested carpet and install it at the requested time.

Deciding if satisfying the demand is right for the enterprise, the carpet salesman calculated a price that allowed Carpet, Inc., to make a profit.

Marshaling the resources of the enterprise to meet the customer's demand, the company teamed with a nylon factory that was able to provide a tailor-made product, its production essentially dictated by Joy Nelson's demands.

Developing and implementing the best approach to the task, Carpet, Inc., collaborated with one of its other business units, a chain of home-decorating stores, to offer value-added services.

Satisfying the customer, Joy Nelson's canary carpet was installed in time for her party. To capitalize on the event, Joy's sales representative was quick to recognize the possibility of a new fashion trend and passed it on internally and to the media.

> By doing only and exactly what each customer required, Hertz discovered that its gold service was less costly to provide than its standard service.
>
> —JAMES H. GILMORE AND
> B. JOSEPH PINE II, *HARVARD BUSINESS REVIEW*

The customer event we portrayed may have the aura of science fiction, but it is actually closer to science fact. The nylon factory described in the scenario is modeled on an actual Solutia plant. In a remarkable piece of kinetics, Monsanto spin-off Solutia is turning its nylon plant into a make-to-order business.

Through complex automation, the plant's business, information, and processing systems are being integrated in ways aimed at allowing customers to order whatever color or kind of nylon they need via the Internet at any time, day or night, including Sunday. The system instantly reserves whatever segment of the nylon stream fits the customer's order. No human hands intervene. Valves open and close, orders are shipped, invoices go out—all electronically and all simultaneously. In essence, the nylon plant's suppliers, processors, and customers are being incorporated as virtually one worldwide organization, a seamless web in which the customers actually set the factory schedule.

Joy Nelson's story illustrates another key aspect of the customer event: It happens immediately; that is, there are none of the usual queues, delays, and downtime as work moves from one worker to the next. Instead, workers throughout the enterprise spontaneously collaborate and interact, focusing on a single customer request.

The kinetic way is not better because it's fast (although it is) but because it's flexible and profitable. When Nelson requested a custom-made carpet and a sales representative specified the fiber color, weight, and texture for the fiber factory, it all happened during one conversation.

Similarly, month-end invoice processing was replaced by a system that calculated the customer's invoice the instant the order was received, and debited the customer's bank account. Month-end management reports were replaced by real-time information updates, so that managers could track performance numbers order by order, customer event by customer event, through the day.

WORKERS DRIVE CUSTOMER EVENTS

At a kinetic enterprise, the real—as opposed to cosmetic—empowerment of workers enables them to constantly meet unpredictable customer demands. At any one time, dozens or hundreds of these events are being played out. As soon as a demand is made, it is pursued, with all the appropriate resources of the organization ready, willing, and able to participate.

The prospect of operating a business that depends almost totally on workers, not managers, and that frees workers to meet customers' unpredictable demands might seem to some a recipe for chaos. It's actually a recipe for success. In the next chapter, we discuss organizing work on the fly.

LIVE THE UNPREDICTABLE

ORGANIZE ON THE FLY

A kinetic business exists in a world of events. Events occur because people are unleashed to organize work as they see fit, to instantly move in unexpected directions, even into brand-new businesses.

A KINETIC enterprise is every bit as unpredictable as the future, because workers organize on the fly. What this means is they think like owners, share common goals and enterprise-wide rewards, disdain constraining job descriptions, design event teams, and learn as they go.

WORKERS THINK LIKE OWNERS

Because kinetic workers see themselves as owners and are personally committed to the enterprise's common performance goals, they are willing to take risks, revamp what they have done in the past, and try new solutions—on the fly.

A true sense of ownership is created only when workers share in the financial rewards of the entire organization's success. At Microsoft, based in Redmond, Washington, workers share in the increasing value of stock. At Palo Alto, California–based Hewlett-Packard, everyone from secretaries to executives receives the same percentage of profit-sharing for the company performance.

• *Case in point:* Kinko's

The ownership mentality that is at the heart of Kinko's corporate culture has been carefully nurtured by founder and chairperson Paul Orfalea. In fact, this commitment to ownership is rooted in Kinko's past. From the beginning, Orfalea shared ownership of the stores with investors in different locations, nearly 130 partners in all. From the beginning it was local ownership, Orfalea insists, that boosted grassroots innovation at Kinko's.

Wherever he travels, and in all his communications, Orfalea emphasizes this sense of ownership. He tells meetings of workers about the day he stopped at a hotel coffee shop and saw a sign by the cash register that read NO CHECKS ACCEPTED OVER $25. He asked the woman behind the counter, "Who made up this silly policy?" She replied, "I don't know. I don't own this place, so ask the owner." At this point Orfalea proclaims to his listeners: "I never want that to happen in Kinko's. All of us have to be owners."

Kinko's culture is built in part on a complete commitment to the concept that everyone is a worker. Orfalea has eliminated the words *employer* and *employee* from Kinko's lexicon. Everyone, from the founder himself to the frontline copy operator, is referred to as a "coworker." Orfalea explains that "employer" is derived from a word that means to bend or mold steel, which is not what Kinko's is all about.

The equality principle is practiced in every aspect of life at Kinko's. There is no special parking in the headquarters lot, for example; if the founder gets there late, he parks in the back. Orfalea and each of his executives work one day a month in a company store, refreshing their frontline connections. A coworker elected by colleagues serves on the board of directors. When a director suggested setting up a nursery to help the working mothers at the headquarters site, it was built pronto.

The sense of ownership is deeply embedded in Kinko's culture and in the respect with which every coworker is treated, regardless of age, experience, or position. In our one-day visit, three different coworkers used the word *democratic* to describe their company. Kinko's approach seems to work.

The founder's belief in joint ownership is reflected in a special compensation program. Part of each coworker's pay is based on the overall performance of his or her particular store, what workers call "a fraction of the action." In addition, Kinko's rewards exceptional performance. All coworkers at a store that comes up with the best performance as measured by sales, profit, and growth criteria receive a trip to Disneyland or Disney World.

Note the contrast with the traditional way in which companies express their appreciation: Instead of rewarding one individual's performance, Kinko's rewards all coworkers in the store that excels at achieving common, enterprise-wide goals. (While the winners are off at Disney, guess who covers for them at the store? The board of directors, of course!) The focus is on making the entire enterprise a success—something any owner would do.

WORKERS SHARE COMMON GOALS AND ENTERPRISE-WIDE REWARDS

Traditionally, the path to success has been well marked and universally understood. You started at or near the bottom, as a junior accountant, say, and gradually moved up the ladder to senior accountant, to accounting department supervisor, and, eventually, to controller, chief financial officer, and executive vice president. At each step along the way your role was clearly laid out. If you carried out your orders efficiently, you could look forward to a promotion and an accompanying raise within a few years.

In kinetic companies geared to events, virtually every aspect of that approach is turned inside out. Instead of forty-five job-grade levels, there may be only four or five titles in the whole company. Workers move from event to event. Pay raises and bonuses are largely tied to their ability to work collaboratively, participating in or leading events to achieve common performance goals.

A manufacturer of customized products, for example, sets

common goals for quality, cost per customized product, and manufacturing speed. If these goals are met, the company will beat its competitors by a broad margin, and everyone in the organization knows the drill.

- *Case in point:* MCI

Many companies use common performance goals to guide workers in designing events. For example, at MCI, the second largest long-distance supplier in the United States (sales of more than $14 billion a year), when a specific goal is set—say, to enter a new telephone market—everyone in the organization begins to work toward creating products and services to achieve that goal. And the culture of the company, based in Washington, D.C., is such that workers experience both tangible and intangible benefits that help to ensure their commitment to the shared goal.

"There's no book that says how to do it," remarks Don Lynch, senior vice president of financial operations for MCI Telecommunications. "We have some tremendously practical people who, because the common goals tend to be very defined, have a tendency to put aside some of their political views or their political self-interest, which I don't think happens in all corporations."

What motivates these workers? "It's sort of the answer to 'Why do people do anything?' " Lynch replies. "I think most people's motivations tend toward 'You have to drive for success' and all that sort of stuff. There are the monetary rewards, but I think it takes a special type of person to work for MCI—

self-motivated, with a strong feeling of self-worth. And you probably get rewarded quicker here than you would other places. Promotions are a function of results, not tenure—and it happens to an awful lot of young people. I was promoted to vice president when I was in my early thirties. That would never have happened in another company."

Workers who produce results get recognition. By leading teams to do things that have never been done before in the process of contributing to the overall success of the organization, they are rewarded with the chance to lead more important initiatives, as well as with higher titles and more pay.

As to management's role in the process, Lynch says, "We communicate very well within the corporation itself. We probably sell internally as well as we sell externally. MCI TV provides direct access to most locations through our own TV network. So senior management has the ability to talk to folks pretty quickly and say, 'Hey, this is where we're going.' "

WORKERS DISDAIN CONSTRAINING JOB DESCRIPTIONS

If workers are to initiate and execute events, they cannot be restrained by hierarchies and pecking orders. There is no room for concerns about who reports to whom or whether the worker in need is putting his or her neck on the line by seeking help from those on higher rungs of the ladder. What counts is the event itself—the challenge, the solution, the implementation.

So a company that would achieve this kind of collaboration

must sweep away the traditional hierarchical barriers to free individual workers to look upon collaboration not as a sign of weakness (the old way of thinking) but as the core strength of the kinetic system. Indeed, once the elements are in place, workers will, on their own, create interlocking networks that reflect their particular needs and interests.

In the old days, the job description for the punch press operator was pretty straightforward: Stand at the machine eight hours a day, five days a week. The operator did nothing other than operate the punch press machine. Job descriptions for workers running the gate shear and the welder were similar. They all mass-produced parts that were stored in a warehouse for later use.

> We're going to have to figure out how to organize people in ways that enable them to coordinate their activities without wasteful and intrusive systems of control and without too much predefinition of what a job is. My own view is that as long as you have a concept called a job, you're asking people to perform to a set of expectations that someone else created. People give more if they can figure out how to control themselves, how to regulate themselves, how to contribute what they can contribute out of their own authentic abilities and beliefs, not out of somebody else's predetermination of what they're going to do all day.
>
> —ROBERT B. SHAPIRO, CHAIRMAN, PRESIDENT, AND CEO, MONSANTO COMPANY, *HARVARD BUSINESS REVIEW*

In a kinetic organization, as a member of a module team, a worker runs the punch press, welds, and assembles parts. She has been cross-trained to continuously redesign the way she works, on the fly. She is always moving around, floating within the module, her job and the way she does it changing with each customer event. If she receives a defective part from another worker on the team, she walks over to the colleague's machine, and they work out the problem on the spot. If the assembly line stops for any reason, the worker goes to the trouble spot to help determine what is needed.

Once a week the punch press operator and other module team members take one hour out to identify ways to reduce time and cost for manufacturing one-of-a-kind products. The worker may join a market event team, which includes new product designers; the team visits customers to determine whether they can create a new product design that can be easily manufactured and better satisfy customers' needs.

• *Case in point:* Aerial Communications

One example of a market event had its start in 1995 when Telephone and Data Systems Inc. (TDS) purchased eight markets in the federal government's auction of the broad-band spectrum for cellular phone service. The company immediately set up a new business to provide six of the markets with personal communications services. Called Aerial Communications and based in Chicago, Illinois, it had eighteen months to build one thousand cell sites and six switching centers.

The schedule was ambitious, but Aerial was designed for

the assignment: It had a flat, kinetic structure with few titles and no offices. Everyone, including the CEO, worked in cubicles. Workers were recruited from diverse backgrounds, but they shared substantial experience in wireless operations, allowing them to contribute immediately. The workers had no job descriptions, only a goal: Launch the new business in eighteen months.

Workers drafted a launch plan that included thousands of steps. Then they developed a list of issues that the company needed to address. Continuous updates were e-mailed to everyone. Workers formed multidisciplinary teams to tackle each issue. On any given day, fifty to one hundred spontaneous teams might be working on issues; some met for a week and disbanded, their tasks done, while others went on for months. Because everyone cooperated to find the right person for each task and to move people from one issue team to another, the fledgling company actually kept its launch plan on track and met its outrageous target.

WORKERS DESIGN EVENT TEAMS

Creating the future can be a high-risk game. Leaders are betting on workers' abilities to generate revenue and profits while facing new challenges. To be successful in a kinetic enterprise, workers must constantly solve problems and implement new ideas.

But fulfilling these requirements is not a one-person task— the more viewpoints, the better. Sometimes all that is required is a quick trip to visit a coworker to get her opinion. More complex problems, however, might require workers to form temporary event teams that try, fail, and learn together. Collaboration with representatives from all disciplines—marketing, sales, manufacturing, distribution, finance, and service—allows workers to get the help they need to execute events. Multidisciplinary teams also benefit from the direct involvement of workers from customer, supplier, and partner companies.

For workers, collaboration on the fly takes some getting used to. These informal event teams appear and dissolve spontaneously, sometimes lasting for minutes or days. Most workers participate in a number of customer and market events at any given time, and they may not even be aware of the others contributing to the event. (The customer advocate coordinates the efforts of the players on a virtual spontaneous team.)

What makes the event possible is the universal understanding that workers will share their expertise when and where it is needed—regardless of whose customers benefit.

> Here's my secret: I don't know what my people are doing, but because I work face to face with them as a coach, I know that whatever it is they're doing is exactly what I'd want them to be doing if I knew what they were doing!
>
> —ANONYMOUS MANAGER,
> QUOTED IN "STOP
> EMPOWERING YOUR PEOPLE:
> THE BEST OF CUTTING EDGE,"
> MANAGEMENT REVIEW

- *Case in point:* **Albert Einstein Healthcare Network**

Above all, leaders of kinetic companies need to instill in their workers the desire to collaborate while making sure they have the ability to do so. That was one of the goals CEO Martin Goldsmith set for himself in 1990. Collaboration was to be the new way of operating, a new shared value. Workers at the Albert Einstein Healthcare Network would learn to access the organization's entire body of expertise to get any job done.

Goldsmith began by spending more than two years reforming his own and his management team's work style to conform to one of the network's stated values—"we rely on each other"—and he admits that it was one of the toughest changes he ever had to make. Goldsmith, like many other leaders, had been quite comfortable calling his own shots. Only after collaboration was embedded in the operations of management did Goldsmith roll out the idea to the entire organization. Einstein then followed up with education and training programs to help every employee adapt. The results of the collaborative work style have been impressive.

At any one time between thirty and eighty interdisciplinary teams are working to reinvent various parts of Einstein's operations. Nurses, for example, are serving on teams designed to create an information-system strategic plan and to develop a new patient care management system. Most of the teams, however, are not large-scale initiatives. They are get-togethers among colleagues intent on finding and offering advice.

For example, Wendy Leebov, the associate vice president

of human resources, gathered a group of colleagues whose work is related to geriatrics and asked: "If you combine all your perspectives, what are we doing in geriatrics, and what does it mean in terms of jobs?" Leebov was surprised at what she learned—and so were the attendees, who found out for the first time what their colleagues were doing in the field of geriatrics.

Leebov calls this kind of spontaneous teaming a huddle. She says, "It's an ad hoc, one-time experience where you pull people together in a huddle about a topic that you need to make decisions on. You get their thinking so you can make the decision in the best way you can." As Leebov points out, "Interdisciplinary teams help people see the integration of different parts of the organization. The huddle concept of getting specific knowledge or input gives employees a lot of flexibility and allows them to move quickly."

To encourage huddling, Einstein uses a low-tech approach. It developed a checklist to get people to think about their entire network of health care providers and colleagues when solving problems or responding to new opportunities. The checklist reads: Ask yourself, Who's affected? Who can help quickly? Who is important to involve? Be sure to think about people at the Medical Center, people from other centers like Belmont and Moss, people from outpatient services, and people from home care partner organizations.

WORKERS LEARN AS THEY GO

Not only does organizing on the fly enable workers to execute events, it also allows them to rapidly accumulate and apply what they have learned.

- ### *Case in point:* Chevron

At Chevron, one of the largest United States–based oil and gas companies, both formal and informal mechanisms help workers stay in touch with experts in all parts of their organization. Some veteran workers, for example, have been assigned to serve as "process masters." They are charged with figuring out which techniques can move from one refinery to another in order to improve quality, save time, and reduce costs. They aren't granted formal authority, but because of their knowledge, workers look to them for advice and innovation.

One of the process masters is Billy Williams, a second-generation refinery worker who has spent eighteen years at the company, which is based in San Francisco, California, and reports revenues of more than $35 billion a year. His specialty is the company's distillation, or crude, units, which are giant cookers that separate crude oil into heavy and light components. Crude units need cleaning about every four years to remove deposits of coke from the unit's pipes. In the past, caked-on coke was burned out of the pipes, a costly process that required furnaces to run at high temperatures for extended periods of time.

In 1994, workers at Chevron's Richmond, California, refinery took a different tack. They tried to clean the crude unit's pipes with the "pig," an abrasive rubber cylinder that moves through the pipes via water pressure. It worked, and at a savings of $1 million per cleaning. Williams's success with the pig allowed him to pass the knowledge on to the El Segundo plant. Now, workers in Salt Lake City are actually designing their new crude unit to make it pig-accessible.

> **If an institution wants to be adaptive, it has to let go of some control and trust that people will work on the right things in the right ways.**
>
> —ROBERT B. SHAPIRO, CHAIRMAN,
> PRESIDENT, AND CEO,
> MONSANTO COMPANY,
> *HARVARD BUSINESS REVIEW*

In addition to the kind of formalized knowledge-sharing exemplified by Williams and the other process masters, Chevron workers have also set up numerous "grassroots networks" for disseminating information. The groups discuss everything from safety to saving money. Some connect through e-mail; some use groupware such as Lotus Notes; and some organize regular meetings, conferences, or forums. Despite the diverse means of communication, each of these groups has a single aim: to share knowledge.

Not only do these networks solve problems, but they also introduce people from one part of the business to those in others. When a worker is tackling an unexpected challenge, he or she knows where to go for expert advice on particular issues —whom to include on the event team.

Chevron's process-masters approach is one way of making the experts and their expertise known. Lotus Notes, which allows workers to set up their own informal knowledge networks, is another. But kinetic-minded organizations have developed a host of techniques for nurturing collaboration. For example, 3M, which reports more than $14 billion in annual revenues, holds yearly conferences and forums to review recent breakthroughs and discoveries. Consulting firms require their consultants to join networks organized according to their expertise, be it technology, strategy, finance, or reengineering. Team members receive calls for help and announcements of breakthrough ideas via electronic and voice mail.

• *Case in point:* Buckman Laboratories International

Although collaboration and networking can exist without it, technology is playing a new role in helping workers form event teams and learn as they go.

Bob Buckman, CEO of Buckman Laboratories, a $270 million chemical company based in Memphis, Tennessee, declares his commitment to collaboration in a *Fast Company* article: An organization "is made up of individuals, each of whom has different capabilities and potentials—all of which are necessary to the success of the company."

In support of that vision, Buckman invested in a company-wide knowledge-sharing network called K'Netix. It is pronounced "kinetics," and not by accident, since any company that would be kinetic must have an electronic network that permits spontaneous worker collaboration and learning. As we have said before, most customer events and market events require real-time cooperation between the customer advocate and other skilled workers.

Buckman is a collaborator's role model. He spends a good deal of his time tuned into the knowledge base. He frequently adds his own suggestions, and he also tackles ideas and complaints on any subject. For instance, one issue was a bonus Buckman presents each year to the salespeople with the largest increase in sales growth. Salespeople across the company and around the country weighed in with their opinions and arguments on the flaws in the existing award system and shared ideas on how to build a more effective system.

K'Netix is a collaboration machine, and Buckman needs it. The company has twelve hundred employees in eighty countries and makes more than one thousand specialty chemicals. That means workers must navigate their way through a torrent of unpredictable customer demands. Buckman does it, in large measure, by giving them the electronic wherewithal to cooperate on one customer event after another, focusing all the company's expertise and knowledge on the problems at hand.

Consider Dennis Dalton, Singapore-based managing director for Asia. One January day at 12:05 P.M., Dalton used K'Netix to ask for help. "We will be proposing a pitch-control program to an Indonesian pulp mill," he wrote, referring to a method to manage tree sap. "I would appreciate an update on successful recent pitch-control strategies in your parts of the world."

By 3:00 P.M. Memphis-based Phil Hoekstra replied, suggesting that Dalton try a particular company product and citing a master's thesis on tropical-hardwood pitch control written by an Indonesian who was studying at North Carolina State University. Over the next few hours Dalton received detailed responses, complete with data, with examples from Canada, Sweden, New Zealand, Spain, Mexico, and South Africa, a total of eleven replies that led directly to a $6 million order.

In the chapter that follows, we define the roles and set forth the attributes of the people who design work on the fly—kinetic workers.

CHAPTER 5

BE THE UNPREDICTABLE

TAP EVERYONE'S ABILITIES

The kinetic enterprise expresses itself in two kinds of complex actions we call customer events and market events. They are not the creation of a bright, forward-looking management team. Rather, they reside in the minds and skills of a special kind of workforce. Events happen because workers make them happen.

IN A kinetic enterprise, everyone is a worker, prepared to play any role at any time. Like the members of a basketball team, kinetic workers understand the game plan or, in our terms, the strategic purpose. They stay alert for the play signals, for insights within the continuous flow of information and advice that circulates within the company. But they get the job done on their own, relying on each other and the skills they have acquired.

In a kinetic enterprise, old notions of predefined jobs and roles, the hierarchical distinctions, no longer exist. Management isn't aligned against staff. Knowledge workers aren't aligned against blue-collar workers. The back office isn't aligned against the front line. Instead, managers actively participate on the front line. All workers roll up their sleeves and operate with real-time information. Everyone interacts directly with customers to satisfy their demands and anticipate their needs. Everyone is wired, connected to everyone else by e-mail and voice mail, eliminating the barriers of distance and time. Even CEOs are workers. At Microsoft (originally Micro-soft), cofounder, chairman, and CEO William H. Gates III spends hours in programmers' offices, brainstorming about the best approach to constructing the code for new software products. At General Motors, plant managers don coveralls to collaborate with workers in solving assembly line problems. At 3M, sales representatives work with their colleagues in manufacturing to solve product quality problems. At Hewlett-Packard, finance experts participate in sales calls.

But is it possible for a company to actually do away with traditional job descriptions and hierarchies? Is it possible for such an organization to operate efficiently and profitably? Consider Oticon, a hearing aid manufacturer located in an old Tuborg soda factory just outside Copenhagen, Denmark. The hearing aid market has been lifeless for years, but Oticon has been the outstanding exception. Since 1990 its operating profits have increased tenfold, and it has been rolling out product innovations at an astounding rate. The difference is Lars Kolind, who in 1988 took over what was then an ailing company and transformed it.

In a *Fast Company* article, Kolind speaks of a future when workers will be "liberated to grow, personally and professionally," and to become "more creative, action-oriented, and efficient." He talks about "thinking the unthinkable," about the organization being its own worst enemy. And he has redesigned his company to match those sentiments, in ways that have a distinctly kinetic ring.

Oticon is no longer organized by department, function, or even business process. All work is based on individual projects, pursued by teams that come together to complete the task and then break up. Anyone with an innovative proposal can lead a project provided he or she can put together a team that can get it done. Kolind wants each of the dozens of ongoing projects to operate like an independent company, and the leaders to "feel like a CEO." Kolind, the official CEO, and his top aides help out when asked, but most decisions, large and small, are made at the project level.

Oticon headquarters looks like a corporate version of Times Square—workers constantly in motion, moving from desk to desk, huddled over computers. Offices are unadorned, since workers don't know where their next project will take them.

For Kolind, that kind of ferment and temporariness is the essence of the successful business. "To keep a company alive," he says, "one of the jobs of management is to keep it disorganized." Freed of old strictures and structures, Oticon and its kinetic workers are ready to take on whatever the unpredictable future holds. They are setting the pace for the momentous changes that are sweeping across the business landscape.

We've talked about what kinetic workers are. What aren't they? For one, they aren't what most of us think of as empowered.

At 3M, CEO Livio DeSimone likes to tell visitors about his

firm rejection of a proposed new product developed by a project team. He says it wasn't appropriate, it was just business for them. But the team didn't give up. It simply went underground, secretly continuing its research until it was able to show DeSimone a product that he could no longer refuse. What was effectively a new generation of materials to make insulated clothing turned into Thinsulate, a major moneymaker for 3M.

The story has many morals, among them a basic principle of the kinetic enterprise: The organization's business is dictated not by the CEO but by the evolving—sometimes stubbornly evolving—expertise of its workers.

And this is where the old notion of "empowered" workers and our kinetic ideas part company. Empowered workers are taught to do what the bosses used to do, while the business stays the same. Kinetic workers, on the other hand, are expected to pull the bosses and everyone else along with them as they constantly evolve the business in response to an ever-changing marketplace.

In this chapter, we set forth the attributes of the kinetic worker. Then we go on to describe the actions of workers as they pursue the organization's strategic purpose and achieve enterprise-wide goals. We start with a portrait of the kinetic worker of the future, a scenario of our own creation.

THE CASE OF SARAH BROWNMILLER

Universal Healthcare is a $2 billion enterprise that encompasses a health plan, a chain of hospitals, and a network of physicians and physician groups. On a frosty March morning in the year 2002, a team of workers, including the CEO and other key senior managers, meets in a twentieth-floor conference room at Universal's Chicago headquarters. The agenda: review a technology strategy crafted by this multidisciplinary team. The strategy will determine in large measure which new information and communications technologies the company will finance over the next three years.

The CEO opens with a spirited summation of Universal's strategic purpose, and Sarah Brownmiller finds herself thinking about her future with the enterprise. Once the technology strategy is in place, she will be free to move on to something else.

Eight years before, Brownmiller, a nurse practitioner, was treating a patient with flulike symptoms who failed to respond to any medication. She called in experts from around the company, and they identified the flulike ailment as an extremely rare disease.

As more and more cases were diagnosed, Brownmiller and her colleagues published their experiences in treating the disease on Universal's intranet. When Universal decided to establish a regional center specifically to care for patients with the illness, Brownmiller was asked to spend a year helping to design the business. She was enthusiastic about the idea, in part because she knew her bonus would grow if she could improve Universal's financial performance.

Then an advance in interactive video communications made it possible for Universal to offer twenty-four-hour electronic home care. Brownmiller leaped at the chance to join the temporary team that was piloting the service. When the project began, she enrolled as a frontline nurse. It was a bureaucratic step down, but it enabled her to act on her holistic medical philosophy and include exercise, nutrition, and stress management as major features of the service. Within twelve months Brownmiller was teaching other nurses how to help distant patients through their daily health care regimens.

It wasn't long before Brownmiller was off on a new tack. A change in state law allowed nurse practitioners to prescribe certain medications, substituting for doctors under some circumstances. Brownmiller had signed up for the extra training required to become certified for this role when she heard that a team within the organization was seeking new ways to enable primary care physicians to see more patients and provide higher quality care. She finagled an invitation to brief the team, urged its members to capitalize on the new capabilities of nurse practitioners—and was invited to join the project.

Three months later the event team set up a nurse practitioner network to provide less expensive care for garden-variety ailments, allowing its physicians to focus on more complex medical problems. Brownmiller joined the network, and as she saw different patients and conditions, she continuously entered her findings into the company's electronic knowledge base and shared her experiences with the national association of nurse practitioners.

When the multidisciplinary team was organized to produce a technology strategy for Universal, Brownmiller was eager to serve. Now, as the team's Chicago meeting is getting under way, she finds herself thinking about the amazing differences between her mother's career and her own. Her mother started as a floor nurse and eventually became head of nursing for a local hospital. Her years of hands-on experience were the perfect qualification for the job. She knew everything about the problems and opportunities her staff faced because, back in those quiescent days, everyone did the same job pretty much the same way it had always been done.

In the twenty-first century, though, careers are not built simply on what you already know. Nor do they progress by moving steadily up some mythical corporate ladder. Kinetic workers look in every direction for new opportunities, learn to tackle unexpected challenges, and risk possible failure as the reasonable price of success. As she sits in the executive conference room, awaiting her turn to tell the CEO what the team will do next, Sarah Brownmiller does not envy her mother's career at all.

THE ROLES OF A KINETIC WORKER

For workers in companies making the transition to kinetics, and for our friend Sarah Brownmiller, customer and market events demand that they play a variety of different roles. Everyone in the enterprise, from CEO to assembly line worker, must be ready to play one or all of them at any given time. These roles are frontline worker, strategist, stakeholder, decision-maker, manager, coach, student, champion, innovator, project member, networker, and leader.

FRONTLINE WORKER

Kinetic workers interact directly with customers to handle unpredictable challenges. Brownmiller, for example, assumed a frontline nursing role to help create the electronic home care service.

STRATEGIST

Kinetic workers understand as well as help shape the strategic purpose and boundaries of the organization. They stay up-to-date on marketplace trends. They understand how their actions affect customers, suppliers, and competitors. Brownmiller recognized the potential importance of the flulike disease and was instrumental in conceiving and establishing a regional treatment center.

STAKEHOLDER

Kinetic workers take personal responsibility for the success of the business. They participate in the rewards that come with the financial success of the total enterprise. With every event Brownmiller strives to improve her own and her colleagues' performance, and she reaps the rewards of that performance.

DECISION-MAKER

Lewis E. Platt, chairman, president, and CEO of Hewlett-Packard Company, with sales of more than $38 billion annually, says, in *Fortune,* that for him, "basically, the whole day is a series of choices." The same holds true for kinetic workers. They use real-time information to read and respond to customer demands and market opportunities. When information is not available, they reach across and beyond their organization for help. Brownmiller, for instance, decided early on to call in experts to help her identify the rare disease. Ultimately, like Platt, kinetic workers make decisions as best they can and learn from the consequences.

MANAGER

There's a saying at Sara Lee: What gets measured is what gets done. Kinetic workers monitor themselves and their teammates, coaching and correcting behavior to improve performance. Brownmiller monitors herself by comparing her patients' outcome data with the results that other nurse practitioners have achieved across the country.

COACH

Kinetic workers help others learn by sharing their experiences, mistakes, and insights, helping others to grow. Brownmiller entered her findings as a nurse practitioner into the company's electronic knowledge base, passed them on to peers in her professional association, and coached anyone who needed help applying her ideas.

STUDENT

Kinetic workers constantly seek to broaden their experience and develop new skills to increase their value to the enterprise. Brownmiller took on extra training to learn the expanded nurse-practitioner role.

CHAMPION

Kinetic workers know how to sell their ideas within the organization, enlisting other workers' support and obtaining needed financial backing. That was Brownmiller's task at the session with Universal's CEO and executive team.

INNOVATOR

Alone and in teams, kinetic workers find new ways to improve current business operations and evolve new customer solutions, new products and services, and new business formats. This often involves taking risks to try out new ideas. For example, Brownmiller became the first to assume an expanded role for nurse practitioners, which led to the increased efficiency of primary care physicians.

PROJECT MEMBER

Kinetic workers collaborate to create new strategies, products, and services. Brownmiller's career is a study in teamwork. She collaborated with colleagues to design and implement the regional center, an electronic home care service, and a technology strategy.

NETWORKER

Kinetic workers build awareness of the work others in the business and industry are doing and cultivate relationships with other workers within and outside the organization. Brownmiller maintained an active relationship with the national association of nurse practitioners, learning from and passing knowledge to other medical professionals.

LEADER

Kinetic workers promote—and serve as role models for—the company's vision, values, and performance goals. As the organization gets more kinetic, workers' leadership role increases, to the point that frontline workers may help set strategic boundaries. Brownmiller took a leadership role at the meeting in Chicago, convincing the CEO and leadership team to invest in their proposed technology strategy.

As kinetic workers play these roles, they take responsibility for their careers, building them event by event. They also fuel the organization as it continuously adapts and evolves its business. The kinetic enterprise relies on the inventive genius of its workers, a force that is largely untapped in traditional organizations. We believe that the ability of companies to nurture this genius and pave the way for its expression is their single most powerful weapon on the business battleground.

> The sad news is, nobody owes you a career. Your career is literally your business. You own it as a sole proprietor. You have one employee: yourself. You are in competition with millions of similar businesses: millions of other employees all over the world. You need to accept ownership of your career, your skills and the timing of your moves. It is your responsibility to protect this personal business of yours from harm and to position it to benefit from the changes in the environment. Nobody else can do that for you.
>
> —ANDREW S. GROVE, CHAIRMAN AND CEO, INTEL CORPORATION, AND AUTHOR, *ONLY THE PARANOID SURVIVE*

Ward Smith, a veteran worker at Haworth Corporation, the office products giant based in Holland, Michigan, has spent the last four years in sales automation. Here's how he describes the kinetic life:

> A person who just wants to do the same thing every day and think about the same process every day will not survive here. No way. I mean, every day I come to work thinking I'm going to be okay, I'm going to be able to sit down and do everything I know best. Inevitably, somebody is going to walk into my office and ask me for something that I have never in my life produced or thought about producing.

The survivors in this organization are going to step up to that plate and attempt it. You may not make it, but you'll do the best you can. Around here, you have to be able to reinvent yourself every other day.

We have seen that workers in kinetic companies take the following steps along that path: They develop new skills as they execute new events, they experiment, and they break the rules.

THE SKILLS OF KINETIC WORKERS

One of the distinguishing traits of kinetic workers is their ability to continually develop new skills in the process of coping with customer and market demands. In other words, they are constantly reinventing themselves—and, in the process, are reinventing their company and its ability to profit from unpredictability.

Sometimes workers reinvent themselves by handling unpredictable events on their own. The sales representative who invents a new selling approach for hospitals, for example, can leverage his past professional experience and skills, and do it all by himself.

Generally speaking, though, an event occurs in the course of a collaboration among a number of workers, and their learning is in an interactive context.

- *Case in point:* **Computer, Inc.**

A new manufacturing system has led an engineer to suggest that her company, which we call Computer, Inc., start creating computers that are exactly tailored to the taste of individual customers. A team with representatives from sales, engineering, and customer service, plus two valued customers has been assembled to invent a new sales approach for this altogether new kind of product.

The team's first decision is a no-brainer: Sales representatives will deal directly and in depth with each customer. No long-distance selling from a price sheet for this product!

The sales representative on the team suggests coaching customers up front on the cost of the various major options. That will enable customers to configure their new computers based on how much they want to spend.

The engineer points out that the sales representatives must be given special training so they will be able to tell customers which custom choices work together, which don't, and why.

A team member from one of Computer, Inc.'s overseas customers reminds the group that some computer designs cannot be supported internationally, and customers should know that before they commit to a final design.

The team comes up with a sales approach, tries it out on some other customers, regroups and redesigns, and then tries again. At each step of the collaboration, the team members further refine the model. By the time the collaboration ends, each member of the team has gained a new understanding of

> **Resolution comes through experimentation. Only stepping out of the old ruts will bring new insights.**
>
> —ANDREW S. GROVE, CHAIRMAN
> AND CEO, INTEL
> CORPORATION, AND AUTHOR,
> *ONLY THE PARANOID SURVIVE*

customers and sales, and how his or her expertise can be applied to that segment of the business.

THE EXPERIMENTS OF KINETIC WORKERS

Worker experimentation is one of the canons of the kinetic enterprise. "Successful failures"—projects that produce important, although not necessarily marketable, results—are expected, accepted, and rewarded. This is so not just because the odds are good that such efforts will occasionally strike pay dirt but because they provide workers with priceless learning experiences. As a 3M executive once put it, "You can only stumble if you're moving."

For many years researchers at 3M have been encouraged to spend 15 percent of their time pursuing projects of particular interest to them, and the company's Genesis Grants provides up to $75,000 in seed money for promising ideas. Actually, 3M often supports individual researcher's projects when no large market potential is evident. The company has discovered literally scores of new products and technologies in that fashion. A niche decorative ribbon product, for example, evolved into other items such as protective face masks, surgical tape, and Scotch Brite cleaning pads. An adhesive coating for a newly introduced DuPont cellophane, developed to solve one customer's need for a moisture-proof tape, led to the launching of Scotch-brand cellulose tape.

- *Case in point:* **Consumer Products, Inc.**

At a company we call Consumer Products, Inc., the technology organization receives funds each year to purchase and experiment with new technology. Seven years ago the picture was very different. When new technology was needed, consultants were brought in to build new computer systems because in-house staff did not have up-to-date skills. When the new systems were implemented, the company spent hundreds of thousands of dollars retraining its staff or, more often, laying off employees with outdated skills and hiring younger college graduates trained in the latest technology.

Today, that money goes to workers who research and pilot new technology before the business's need for it is identified. They scan the technology horizon for promising new developments, and when they spot a spark of light in the distance, they pounce.

At any one time the workers are running a variety of new technology experiments, from testing new operating systems on their own desktop computers to designing multimedia programs to learning the art of multimedia design. The in-house staff knows more about the realities of new technologies than do many of the people selling the products. They beta-test products for vendors and create test applications for their own department's use so they can see the new technology perform under the stress of a real business environment. The technology department's experiments with leading-edge processes—perhaps viewed by some in the company as impractical and unusable when they were begun—have led to more than a dozen strategic uses of new technology over the past seven years.

What is true for the technology side of this kinetic company is true for the human resources, accounting, and supplier-relations areas as well. All parts of the organization benefit from mechanisms that urge workers to try out new ideas.

THE RULES AND KINETIC WORKERS

Once unleashed, a kinetic worker's drive is not easily controlled, nor should it be. Bob Milstead, director of manufacturing for Haworth, learned the hard way. He oversees more than twenty-five hundred employees who are organized into roughly 250 teams. One day Milstead went down to the factory floor and told the workers that there were some changes he wanted to make. He said that the changes would improve the efficiency of the steel plant and that the workers would come to really like them.

Milstead was sitting in his office a few days later when a group of factory people walked in and, without a word, unplugged his phone and moved it to a different table. Then they took some papers from his desk and placed them somewhere else, and they also moved his bookcase. As they left they said, "There, that will work a lot better." As Milstead tells the story: "The point they made to me was, 'Hey, don't come down and tell us that we're going to like this a lot better. We know how we have to do our work.' It was well taken. I wasn't offended by it at all. In fact, I thought it was great."

> **When people get a chance to accomplish something themselves, they just come to life.**
>
> —ANTHONY RUCCI, CHIEF
> ADMINISTRATIVE OFFICER,
> SEARS, ROEBUCK & CO.,
> *FORTUNE*

In kinetic enterprises, managers not only have to let workers carry the ball but at times they also have to celebrate a worker's aggressiveness in pursuing his or her research—even when management has said no.

• *Case in point:* Microsoft

At Microsoft, Nathan Myhrvold, chief technology officer ("chief propeller head," in the language of *Fortune*), lived deep inside the company's operating systems group where a constant battle ensued over which of two models should be used in the next generation of operating systems. When Myhrvold lost, he organized a few people to dig up research that would demonstrate the usefulness of his approach; with the research in hand, he was able to reverse the decision.

Myhrvold knew that if his guerrilla tactics produced results, he would be listened to at Microsoft; this would not necessarily be the case elsewhere. What has helped Microsoft flourish (it's the world's number one independent software company with sales of more than $11 billion a year) is the willingness of its leaders to allow workers to break the rules, and accept occasional failure as the price of success. Its guiding philosophy, to paraphrase Robert Browning: Let your reach exceed your grasp.

PART 2

THE JOURNEY

FOLLOW FIVE CONCURRENT PATHS TO CORPORATE KINETICS

INTRODUCTION

IN THE previous chapters we sought to answer the what and why questions: Why is a new corporate model so urgently needed? Just what is the kinetic approach, and what does it have to offer? In the chapters that follow we address the how question: How should companies go about their journey toward a kinetic future?

The answer leads us along five separate paths, although in the real world organizations must travel them concurrently. We examine the role of the leader; the creation of the kinetic workforce; the development of process, technology, and facilities infrastructure; and the operation of all these components in igniting and pursuing customer events and market events.

As we shall see, the trip starts with the leaders and their executive cadres who are responsible for setting the strategic purpose and boundaries. They also establish the protocols whereby a kinetic workforce is hired and/or trained. Financial and emotional motivations must be devised to foster an entirely new attitude among workers toward their jobs and their organizations. But once that workforce is in place and has started piloting events, leaders must learn to resist the familiar temptation to micromanage. The evolution of the kinetic workforce comes with the experience of pursuing events.

In these chapters we show how organizations are designing processes, technologies, and facilities to help workers across the enterprise work simultaneously and spontaneously. The purpose: to make it possible for leaders and workers alike to approach the outrageous goal of acting in zero time.

In most organizations that have made the shift toward a kinetic model, the process has been gradual. It is clearly a demanding effort. In fact, it only occurs when the leaders of organizations admit that, given the state of the business world and of their own businesses, they have no choice.

You may not feel that you are anywhere close to that point as yet, but we would urge you to at least hedge your bets. The underpinnings of the old predictable mass-market paradigm are crumbling. Join us for the exhilarating journey.

CHAPTER 6

THE FIRST PATH

CREATE THE NEW LEADERSHIP

How do you devise a strategic purpose that will inspire workers to shoot the moon? How do you set boundaries while inspiring workers to challenge them? You lead from the front line while making decisions in real time.
Here's how.

IN TRADITIONAL, task-based organizations, leaders are, by definition, separate and removed from their workers. Leaders are responsible for predicting market trends from year to year, developing strategies to take advantage of them, and making sure the strategies are implemented.

The message trickles down the chain of command, from boardroom to division to department to workstation. The vice president of sales must sell enough products or services to meet the revenue forecast. The vice president of operations must scale production or service facilities to meet customer demand and stay within the projected operating costs. The head of customer service must do the best she can to support new customers while staying within her department's budget.

In companies organized by process, leaders have similar roles: They set the course and sit atop the managerial apparatus that puts their decisions into effect. That double mission has never been all that easy, but in many industries nowadays it has become grueling and frustrating as customer demands have fragmented and new markets have emerged. The demands heaped on corporate leaders are constantly escalating.

Seiko, for example, is turning out 5,000 separate and distinct watch models. That means company leaders must predict customer demand, scale manufacturing facilities to accommodate that forecast, and meet revenue and cost estimates for all 5,000 models—a monumental task.

The leaders of deregulated industries face an even more daunting prospect. Bert Roberts, MCI's president, has predicted that half of the company's operating revenues in the year 2000 will come from divisions that did not even exist in 1995. So leaders at MCI and companies like it will have to forecast sales, scale operations, and meet revenue and cost estimates in areas where they have little or no experience.

In essence, that is the kind of future for which the kinetic approach prepares you. In the kinetic enterprise, leaders still predict and implement winning plays to succeed in visible markets. But they also prepare themselves and their organization to respond to the invisible, unpredictable market shifts that have become so commonplace in the modern business world.

In this chapter we show how leaders can create self-adapting, self-renewing companies that are organized for instant action. We detail the five key tasks of kinetic leaders: (1) set the company's strategic purpose, (2) establish boundaries within which that purpose may be pursued, (3) provide mechanisms whereby workers can challenge those boundaries, (4) champion market and customer events, and (5) make decisions in real time.

But of course there is another, earlier stage of the process— the actual decision to undertake a kinetic journey and live by its two outrageous goals. In fact, the announcement of those goals —to serve a single customer and act in zero time—is the necessary first step in launching the new enterprise. The goals challenge workers to reinvent themselves and the infrastructure of their business to execute fast, profitable events. They make it clear that today's static business design will no longer suffice, that workers must begin to think about strategies, operations, and technology in brand-new ways.

What's more, the goals bear a message that is the very essence of the whole system: The kinetic journey is never over. It is a continuum of ever new ideas and ever better solutions, one after another, always approaching but never quite achieving perfection. More than any other, this is the message that leaders must convey to their workers again and again and again.

Consider Custom Foot, serving markets of one by combining modern technologies and a network of craftsmen in Italy to produce inexpensive made-to-order shoes in a few weeks. Impressive, but a few weeks is still a few weeks. In the quest for zero time, the company's twenty-first-century workers will undoubtedly have new and better ideas—maybe a chain of one-hour shoe stores, with desk-size factories that can cut and sew a pair of shoes while a customer waits.

Sound impossible? So did the whole Custom Foot formula a few years ago. Outrageous goals inspire outrageous achievement.

SET STRATEGIC PURPOSE

In a traditional organization, leaders define the specific roles in departments and processes that workers will play. In the kinetic enterprise, leaders set a new, unbounded charter for workers. They challenge workers to do whatever it takes—reinvent themselves, their role, and their business—to bring the strategic purpose to life.

At Microsoft the strategic purpose is "Information at your fingertips." This is Bill Gates's description from his book, *The Road Ahead,* of what that means and the universe in which his company should be operating:

> Imagine a marketplace or an exchange. Think of the hustle and bustle of the New York Stock Exchange or a farmer's market or a bookstore full of people looking for fascinating stories and information. All manner of human activity takes place, from billion-dollar deals to flirtations. Many transactions will involve money, tendered in digital form rather than currency. Digital information of all kinds, not just as money, will be the new medium of exchange in

this market. The global information market will be huge and will combine all the various ways human goods, services, and ideas are exchanged.

The "information" of Microsoft's strategic purpose suggests benefits that current customers have never received or probably imagined. It is not tied to a specific technology, business, or market; rather, it is intended to leave the door open for workers' innovations.

At Toyota the strategic purpose is to lead in the convergence of telecommunications, information, and automotive technology. For Susumu Miyoshi, a Toyota director in charge of telecommunications, that translates into a strategy that offers an outrageous customer benefit for Toyota customers: "Anything you can do at home, you can do while in motion."

In the Miyoshi future, multimedia devices will tell drivers which parking lots are full, show them on electronic maps the least-congested route to their destination, and describe what is playing at a local movie theater.

The strategic purpose at Toyota is not geared to specific car designs. It directs workers toward developing new competencies and reacting rapidly as new technologies and markets emerge.

As a result of this strategy, the company, almost unnoticed, has been ringing up telecommunications sales of close to a billion dollars a year, calculated on the basis of its percentage of ownership in various firms. It has interests in three major Japanese telecommunications businesses: a domestic long-distance company, a mobile phone company, and an overseas long-distance company. The automaker also owns equity stakes in thirty-six other telecommunications, cable television, broadcasting, and satellite television companies, which means it has ties to virtually every element of the telecommunications industry.

By championing a strategic purpose, leaders of kinetic enterprises challenge workers to evolve current product offerings, reinvent their own skills, see the whole business picture, and create discontinuities that can yield competitive advantage. Leadership teams formulate the strategic purpose and then spend considerable time communicating and interpreting it for workers. This allows workers to innovate beyond the visible horizon.

SET STRATEGIC BOUNDARIES

Yes, kinetics demands that leaders unleash workers to achieve a strategic purpose. Also required, though, are clear rules of the game to make sure that all workers' actions contribute to competitive advantage and financial success. Boundaries must be set.

To begin with, leaders must clearly define what markets or businesses are outside the strategic domain.

At Intel, for example, the strategic purpose has long been to be the building-block supplier to the computer industry worldwide. One of the strategic boundaries has been: We will not enter any business being served by a customer.

At Sears the strategic domain is embodied in the definition of its target customer: a family with an annual income of between $25,000 and $60,000 that either owns its own home or has children living at home, or both, in which the female is the principal shopper and is between the ages of twenty-five and fifty-four.

Efforts by workers—known as "associates" at Sears—to serve customers outside the target area are frowned upon. Ideas to make retail centers more in line with target customers are encouraged. In one Latino and Christian neighborhood, an associate brought in religious jewelry that he knew would boost store visits and sales. In another city a team of associates is piloting home-delivery service. In another location an associate brings in colorful fashions suited to local tastes.

Leaders must also set boundaries requiring that the bottom line be served. The business case for any new idea must demonstrate a positive impact on performance and profits. And performance should be measured by concrete standards such as customer retention, revenue growth, or shareholder value.

There can hardly be a broader strategic purpose statement than that of Thermo Electron, the $3 billion technology specialist headquartered in Waltham, Massachusetts: "to develop technological solutions to society's problems." With this wide-open strategic domain, the company makes dozens of products, everything from power plants to artificial hearts to laser hair-removers. But most are made not by the headquarters company but by some twenty-one publicly traded spinouts that orbit the organization. We will hear more about Thermo Electron in due course, but suffice it to say that the company's strategic purpose demands innovation of its workers, and it gives them the ultimate incentive—a chance to pilot an event into a new spinout. Ideas rain down thick and fast, but the sorting and sifting process is stringent.

Thermo spinouts may not compete with each other or the parent company; each new spinout must create a brand-new family niche. That makes it possible for spinouts to work together on the technology for new products, often with the help of Thermo's central research division. It allows the organization to develop an integrated labor market so that more employees can move from spinout to spinout.

In addition, the business case for a new spinout must meet exacting financial standards to assure commercial viability and more. To escape the nest, fledglings must show the ability to grow at least 30 percent a year.

ENABLE WORKERS TO CHALLENGE STRATEGIC BOUNDARIES

As vital as strategic boundaries are to success, the kinetic enterprise makes provision for and even encourages challenges from workers. To managers in traditional organizations that may sound like heresy, an open invitation to chaos, the suggestion box gone ballistic. But particularly in organizations so dependent on workers' innovations and initiative, leaders must take every opportunity to correct or eliminate a boundary that has outlived its usefulness.

Just how much importance kinetic leaders give this ability to challenge strategic boundaries is evident in our story about Intel in chapter 2. Intel chose not to enter any business currently served by its customers, including computer manufacturers such as IBM. In one instance CEO Andy Grove was persuaded to set this strategic boundary aside. A year after he made the decision, Grove demonstrated the new chip and bus design, and was hailed by all major computer manufacturers.

Paul Orfalea's strategic vision is "to be to the eye what the telephone company is to the ear." The strategic boundary: Provide office services, in a copy-store format, that meet customer needs and increase profits. But coworkers are allowed to push the boundaries of what a copy store offers by making suggestions for new product offerings.

This strategic combination of virtually unbounded innovation and clear boundaries, coupled with workers' abilities to challenge these boundaries, has allowed Kinko's to grow and evolve from traditional copy store to post office, videoconferencing center, passport photographer, PC renter, and more, with strong financial performance.

CHAMPION MARKET AND CUSTOMER EVENTS

It isn't enough for leaders to develop a strategic purpose and strategic boundaries. They must promote and interpret these two guiding lights of the kinetic way, encouraging and participating directly in the exchange of ideas. Leaders must also serve as model kinetic workers championing their own events and participating in events led by other workers.

At Kinko's, CEO Paul Orfalea spends weeks each year traveling around the United States. At a stop in Portland, Oregon, not long ago, he spoke about the strategic purpose to a group of three hundred coworkers. The meeting lasted from 9:00 A.M. to noon, with Orfalea explaining his philosophy and telling down-home stories to bring the ideas to life. True to Kinko's style, while frontline workers attended the session, managers handled customers at the stores.

Eager to tap workers' ideas, Orfalea lectures his coworkers on the importance of every idea, both big and small. And he participates directly in the idea-exchange process, using the company's voice mail system to spread workers' ideas.

In a typical day Orfalea receives a dozen ideas from workers in his voice mailbox. They can range from a new antivirus program to a debate over a new color copier technology to how stores should measure waste. He forwards the best ideas, with his own thoughts, to Kinko's management at approximately 900 stores. Managers reply, and the CEO broadcasts the best replies as well.

Idea exchange is part of the company's culture, part of everyday life, and takes many forms. On Fridays at headquarters, Orfalea and his coworkers meet in the lunchroom and pass around a microphone to share their latest thoughts and ideas. Whatever the form of exchange, the ideas are taken seriously.

When leaders participate in the exchange of ideas, they send a powerful message throughout the enterprise: There are no exceptions to the kinetic call for commitment and engagement.

Michael Dell, the founder of Dell Computer Corporation, champions his own events. One morning in the spring of 1997, his first stop of the day was a visit with the team that put the company on a Web site, where it was at that point already selling $1 million worth of computers a day. Dell tossed off his ski parka and plowed into a discussion on how to pump up sales even more. He wanted Web pages tailored for corporate customers to order online. And he was impatient for a new feature that would dash off a digital confirmation to customers within five minutes of placing an order, a way of reassuring buyers that all was well.

When Michael Dell first proposed selling PCs on the Web, some members of his senior staff were skeptical. They doubted that a market would ever materialize. Nevertheless, convinced of the rightness of his cause, he continued to champion the project within the company, eventually overcoming the objections. It was the kind of dedication Dell wanted from all his workers, and he was showing the way.

MAKE DECISIONS IN REAL TIME

In a corporation dedicated to flexibility and rapid, targeted response, leaders can't dillydally. It would defeat the whole purpose. In the collaborative, simultaneous rush of a customer event or market event, there is no time for participating leaders to slow down, check all the angles, or "sleep on it." They must be plugged into what is happening and have sufficient confidence in their workforce to sign off quickly on decisions they once agonized over.

Wired into the company, constantly gathering information about ongoing projects, and entertaining reactions and suggestions from the workers, kinetic executives lead and make decisions in real time.

In traditional companies, for example, when workers

awaken to a negative radio report about their industry or company, their feelings of confusion or embarrassment can color the whole day or the next week. The most they can expect is a brief article in the monthly employee newsletter. At Kaiser Permanente, the response comes fast, in real time, and sometimes from Dr. David Lawrence, the CEO. By the time Kaiser workers arrive at their jobs on such a day, Lotus Notes already carries a message from Dr. Lawrence or his communications staff acknowledging the story, spelling out programs already under way to solve the problems raised in the report.

Here's a typical update from Dr. Lawrence: "Good news: After months of HMO bashing in the press, the latest issue of *Newsweek* has published a supportive article." He comments on the article and congratulates the people responsible. He reports that Kaiser received the highest ratings from the National Committee for Quality Assurance and other accreditation organizations. He cites a positive mention in *Consumer Reports* magazine and then goes on to comment on what competitors are doing—a matter of continuing concern to kinetic workers. He ends by pointing out some areas where the organization still has work to do. He uses the forum to inform, acknowledge, and keep employees focused on Kaiser's strategic purpose and where Kaiser is headed.

The kinetic corporation depends on real-time communication and real-time trust. Whether they are championing their own market events, like a Michael Dell, helping out with a customer event, or simply studying a business proposal, leaders must learn to respond within the flow of a project. That means truly accepting the risks that are inherent in the kinetic system.

In the old corporate model, the assumption was that the leaders, with their superior brainpower and education, knew what should be done and how it should be done. Kinetics is intended for a business world where that approach is no longer viable, where corporations must rely on the initiative and decision-making of the workers as a whole. And that requires a fundamental change in the attitudes of the leaders, a new feeling of confidence that will allow them to accept at face value, and promptly, the judgments of their worker-partners.

We are not suggesting that this is an easy or comfortable role for a leader accustomed to hands-on management. We are not saying that it will happen overnight. We are saying that it is necessary and inevitable. In an organization that marches in real time, the leaders must be in step.

Although we have discussed a number of the key tasks of the kinetic leader in this chapter, including the setting of both strategic purpose and strategic boundaries, much remains to be said on the topic. But we will encounter it again in the pages ahead as we see leaders taking part in customer and market events and interacting with their kinetic workers in pursuit of the outrageous goals of serving a single customer and acting in zero time.

At this point you may find yourself wondering just how this paragon of a workforce, capable of shouldering responsibility for the entire enterprise, can be put together. That is the subject of our next chapter.

CHAPTER 7

THE SECOND PATH

BUILD THE RIGHT WORKFORCE

How do you create an enterprise that can organize on the fly? Prepare workers to do the job. Here's how.

IN THE hunt for a kinetic workforce, organizations have taken two divergent paths. New or growing businesses primarily focus on snaring new workers already equipped with kinetic abilities. Established or stable businesses seek to help existing employees recognize and develop kinetic skills.

HIRE KINETIC

In traditional companies, job interviews are concerned with the candidate's specific skills and experience. Kinetic organizations search for candidates who have innate talents rather than just track records, and their attitudes and personalities must match the corporate culture.

The underlying assumption: As the world becomes less and

less predictable, past experience is less and less relevant to future performance. Any specific skills that are missing can be learned. Mind-sets are harder to absorb. Microsoft and Southwest Airlines set the pace for what it means to hire kinetic.

MICROSOFT

In 1993, Microsoft cofounder and CEO Bill Gates told his software developers, "There's not a single line of code here today that will have value in, say, four or five years' time." That rapid perishability means that Microsoft employees must be capable of rapidly absorbing new ideas and new skills in the process of continuously producing new solutions. That takes outstanding intelligence and creativity, qualities that Gates calls "relatively innate." And he believes they can best be found among freshly minted college graduates. In its pursuit of just the right employee, Microsoft receives something like 120,000 résumés a year, many from vastly skilled and experienced developers. Only a lucky few get the interview. The average age of its workers in 1994 was thirty-one.

Some of the other qualities Microsoft looks for in a new hire: the ability to ask insightful questions, to see connections between disparate domains of knowledge, and to collaborate with colleagues. Those who make the grade must also be so well versed in programming structures that they comprehend long printouts of code in an instant. They are expected to think about the code constantly.

Microsoft offers candidates distinctly lower salaries than

those dangled by competitors. Instead, employees receive stock option packages that can yield huge payouts if the company prospers. In fact, analysts have estimated that more than two thousand software developers in Microsoft's class of 1989 became millionaires in just two years.

Those people who are willing to make the trade-off and take the risk, betting on the company's future and their own role in it, are just what Gates ordered. No need to untether these workers from the constraints of the traditional business approach—they were born kinetic.

SOUTHWEST AIRLINES

Of the 124,000 people who apply for jobs at Southwest Airlines each year, only about 5,000 are hired. Southwest CEO Herb Kelleher wants people who can continually respond to customers and reinvent the company, and he has some very specific qualities in mind for the chosen few. At the top of the list is a sense of humor, followed closely by unselfishness. "We look for . . . people with a sense of humor who don't take themselves too seriously," Kelleher says, according to *Nuts!: Southwest Airlines' Crazy Recipe for Business and Personal Success,* by Kevin and Jackie Freiberg. Southwest will train newcomers in the details of the airline business, but Kelleher doesn't want to waste time trying to change people's inherent attitudes.

Why the emphasis on a sense of humor? Kelleher sees it as the perfect antidote for the stresses associated with hard work in an extremely competitive environment. Giving employees the freedom to be themselves, and enjoy what they're doing in the process, attracts workers who will naturally go the extra mile to provide what Colleen Barrett, the executive vice president for customers, calls POS (Positively Outrageous Service).

Southwest wants natural self-starters who are not afraid to take risks, and that includes a willingness to challenge the status quo. Workers are expected to make decisions on their own, without fear of retribution if something goes wrong. Bureaucracy is anathema.

To keep its high-energy workers challenged, Southwest links its major financial rewards to the company's profit-sharing plan. The airline invested almost $54 million in its profit-sharing plan in 1995.

To guide its liberated workers in the right direction, Southwest seeks to foster a we're-all-in-this-together culture. Workers are kept informed of operations company-wide and how their own and others' jobs fit into the pattern of the organization as a whole. The people flying the planes understand the jobs of the people unloading the bags and fueling the jets. The goal: to stimulate communication and innovation across internal boundaries.

Southwest also educates workers on the basic realities of its business—the number of customers the company needs to make a profit, for example. And to keep the sense of urgency high, the company publishes monthly industry rankings that plot Southwest's scores against those of its competitors for on-time performance, baggage handling, and customer complaints.

- *Insight:* **Hire for innate talent.**

Microsoft puts its emphasis on IQ, creativity, and other "relatively innate" talents when it searches for new employees. Other kinetic organizations put the emphasis elsewhere—on candidates' eagerness to take on new challenges and risks, on big-picture thinking, on the ability to handle paradox and ambiguity, on resilience under fire. In an unpredictable world, what counts is raw brain power, drive, and the ability to operate effectively in chaos. The rest can be learned.

- *Insight:* **Hire for attitude.**

Companies driving to become kinetic look for attitude. They hire people who think like owners. Bill Gates and Herb Kelleher built their companies to break the rules of their industries, and they needed people who could rewrite the rule books, people with a thirst for responsibility and ownership.

The only way to attract and retain these workers was to make them an offer they couldn't refuse, a package of extraordinary rewards and opportunities. The compensation packages were potential blockbusters that enabled workers to share in the financial rewards of success. What's more, the candidates were given the chance to invent their own jobs and careers at the same time that they invented the future of their companies —in an environment that was more cooperative than competitive, more democratic than autocratic. That opportunity, to be at the decision-making heart of an organization, is what attracts the innately kinetic job applicants.

- *Insight:* **Hire what you need.**

Microsoft is a manufacturer, Southwest is a service company, and each has developed its own special screening techniques to test employment candidates.

At Microsoft, applicants are asked how they feel about a number of ideas and issues. If the answer is anything like "I don't know" or "I have to think about it," the applicant flunks. Bill Gates insists on people who can express an opinion and exchange ideas on the spot, a skill critical to team learning and innovation.

At Southwest, each applicant is asked to give a five-minute presentation in front of a roomful of other applicants and is given ample time to prepare. Those who work on their own presentations instead of listening to the speakers are out. Kelleher insists on people who are thoughtful of others and concerned about being seen to be thoughtful—an attitude critical to working in a service business.

PREPARE WORKERS TO ACT KINETIC

Not every business with kinetic ambitions is able to hire a new, kinetic workforce. The challenge: Help current workers make the kinetic mind-shift. The pacesetters are Albert Einstein Healthcare Network, the state of Kentucky, and Haworth, Inc. Each of these kinetic pioneers prepares its workers in multiple ways to act kinetic.

ALBERT EINSTEIN HEALTHCARE NETWORK

Seven years ago, Martin Goldsmith, CEO of the Albert Einstein Healthcare Network of Philadelphia, admitted to himself that his organization lacked the adaptability it would need to prosper in the uncertain, rapidly evolving health care marketplace. Einstein's competitors were developing profitable alternatives to traditional hospital care, including outpatient services, home care, and even disease prevention programs that could help patients avoid hospitals altogether. Cost-cutting alone could not keep hospitals afloat.

To meet the challenge, Goldsmith developed a new organizational strategy. He began to build a network of companies that could provide a complete spectrum of care, including primary care physicians, hospital services, outpatient services, home care, nursing homes, rehabilitation centers, educational programs, and more. But he didn't stop there. He knew his competitors would continue to innovate and that Einstein's workforce would have to learn to exploit new care formats, new disease management techniques, and new drug therapies.

So Goldsmith formulated a new strategic purpose for his workers. In the past they had been asked to keep Einstein in the forefront of acute-care hospitals, measured by the number of beds filled. Their new goal was to raise the health status of patients, measured by the improved health of individual patients. Instead of simply going about their predefined tasks, they would have to do whatever it took to achieve the new strategic purpose, whether it meant moving an elderly patient out of the hospital into home care or establishing a nutrition regimen to keep a diabetic out of the hospital.

Despite these major changes, Goldsmith was determined to prevent them from affecting the warmth and sense of mission that had made the hospital so successful in the past. And he intended to do whatever was necessary to prepare existing workers for a kinetic environment rather than making wholesale staffing changes.

He knew it would not be easy. The organization's culture was accepting and paternalistic. Half of the employees had fifteen or more years of service, and 75 percent of the executives had at least twenty years. They were comfortable, easygoing, risk-averse, and set in their ways.

The transformation process started at the top with the organization's leaders. This phase, which took two years, got under way with the preparation of the following set of values that would henceforth govern everyone's actions:

- We are compassionate.
- We are totally dedicated to our patients and their families.
- We are enthusiastic, energetic, and hardworking.
- We demonstrate drive, spirit, and initiative in pursuit of our mission.
- We are confident in our tradition of success and leadership in our field.
- We are loyal to our organization and our values.
- We insist on ever-higher quality.
- We take responsibility and make things work.

- We attend to the details.
- We recognize and celebrate excellent performance.
- We take pride in our work, because we know that quality is not accidental.
- Professionalism is our hallmark.
- We always present a welcoming, polished image.
- We show respect for cultural differences and the dignity of each individual.
- We strive to put others at ease and to communicate in ways they can understand.
- We make hospitality and responsiveness to patients and each other a habit, adding warmth to our environment.
- We rely on each other.
- We promote trust through our honest transactions.
- We show respect for the work and ideas of others.
- We express our appreciation and thanks for each other's contributions.
- By giving our support and cooperation, we make each other stronger.

Goldsmith recruited Janine Kilty, currently senior vice president, AEHN, to assist with the transformation. She helped him organize meetings of his executive team away from headquarters. They were attended by all the leaders of the network—the chief operating officer, the chief financial officer, the physician responsible for planning, the head of human resources, the general counsel, and the heads of rehabilitation, psychiatry, geriatrics, and support services. The written values were reviewed at these meetings, and the leadership team was divided into three-person groups to figure out how the values could be applied.

At one point the CEO himself was put on the spot. Goldsmith was told he would have to adopt a more team-oriented approach and accept the need for appropriate confrontations with his management group. He demanded specifics: "Fine. Let's talk about what it would look like and how it would be different."

Back at the office, the members of the leadership team practiced living by the set of values. They moved from "long-distance" management and communications to more personal, collaborative approaches, not only among themselves but with subordinates as well. "We began to see people working together as they need to be," Kilty says.

It soon became clear to everyone that Goldsmith was deadly serious about the transformation. When a few managers refused to accept the values and failed to move to a collaborative work style, they were handed their walking papers. Senior managers' performance today is judged in large measure on their success in adopting kinetic behaviors. Goldsmith's obvious commitment to kinetic values and his determination to transform the organization have been prime factors in mobilizing his staff.

To bring the transformation message to all workers, Einstein's management launched a major communications program through meetings, newsletters, and bulletin boards. Workers were brought up to date on the managed-care market, moves by competitors, and new developments in their local health care marketplace. The goal: to help them understand why they and their company would have to change continually to keep up with their dynamic industry.

Teams of workers were organized to figure out how to implement the values. They called for new kinds of training programs, the realignment of reward and recognition programs, and the creation of monitoring mechanisms so that employees could see how they were doing.

The company provided a host of new programs to assist in training and retraining. The choice of programs to attend—and the decision as to whether or not to attend at all—rested with the individual workers. Einstein made it clear, however, that new competencies would be needed, and those who failed to obtain them would have little or no job security.

At newly created assessment centers, trained counselors sat down with individual workers to review strengths and weaknesses, and prepare a personal development plan. The results of the assessment were private, and career coaching was available if needed. Workers could also opt to go through the assessment process with a peer team of their own choosing. After completing a set of tasks, team members were given the tools they needed to rate their own performances.

Today's portfolio of clinics, workshops, and courses at Einstein bears more than a passing resemblance to an MBA curriculum. One twelve-week course helps workers with their reading comprehension and computation skills. Another explains the workings of the managed-care market, locally and nationally, and suggests what the staff can do to help the company win in the marketplace. Some of the offerings seek to improve the interpersonal skills so vital to kinetic success—public speaking, for example, or assertiveness training. Another focuses directly on "dealing with change."

Worker enrollment in these courses is high, and the enthusiasm for continued education is also reflected in the growth of Einstein's tuition reimbursement program. "People are focused on accessing whatever they can to add to their work portfolio," says Kilty. "I would say that's true of nine out of ten people who work here."

Wendy Leebov, Kilty's associate, comes into contact with hundreds of workers a week. When she was asked recently about the workers' reaction to the many changes, she replied, "People are feeling pretty good." But, she admitted, the passage had not been easy. "When you're unfit physically and you start to exercise, every step you run, every weight you lift, and every lap you swim is exhausting," she said. "You want to cry because of the degree of effort. But after you start to develop new muscle, there's much less strain on you when you reach some of those new plateaus. There's a kind of fitness, and I think people here have gone through that."

KENTUCKY

This state is reengineering more than twenty business processes in such departments as transportation, health services, families and children, agriculture, libraries, justice, and environmental protection. But the massive program has a kinetic twist. It is being led from the front line by the workers themselves. More than 250 have been trained to redesign work, and they have proven the value of the concept by piloting a series of "quick-win" initiatives.

Governor Paul Patton is the guiding genius of a program called "Empower Kentucky." He demonstrated his kinetic inclinations early in his first term by embracing a new way to operate, focused on competency, collaboration, and trust. And to show his commitment to those goals, he abandoned the customary practice of hiring close friends and supporters to head cabinet-level departments; instead, he appointed an independent committee, which conducted an intensive search for people who could lead the kind of responsive organization he had in mind. As a result, the Democratic governor's cabinet leaders—senior business, legal, and education executives—include five Republicans. The selection of his new cabinet sent a signal to workers all over the state: Competence counts more than politics.

Kentucky went on to build a foundation for worker-led events, and education was the cornerstone. A program was developed to teach workers how to analyze their own processes, redesign their own operations, and apply new technology.

Management of state departments had always changed with each election, and plans for improving department operations had always changed with them. So state workers had a habit of ignoring each improvement scheme, knowing that it was strictly temporary. The governor's vote of confidence in workers scrambled those preconceptions. Once they realized that they were going to be given a chance to serve as their own event champions, workers realized they would be able to revamp operations to meet long-term goals as well as short-term challenges.

Those feelings of confidence were boosted when Governor Patton convinced the legislature to commit $103 million to the program, up front and before any specific project had been selected. And to keep the workers informed about the program, the state established a newsletter that regularly reported on workers' innovations; it is distributed to every state worker and is available on the state's public Web site. Along with the Web site, public television shows and town hall meetings enable the public as a whole to follow the reinvention of local government services.

The public Web site actually carries more than simple updates. Event teams put their assessment documents, design plans, and project plans on the site so that workers in every agency can examine emerging best practices and apply them in their own bailiwicks. To make sure the dozens of events are in cahoots as new computer systems and business processes are designed, the state created uniform technology and design standards. Workers are trained in the standards so that each new computer system builds on its predecessors, and one system talks to another.

The careful preparation and worker enthusiasm delivered impressive results. In the first 180 days of the program, government workers put in place more than fifty ideas to save money and improve customer service. This, despite the fact that the members of most teams had never worked together before.

HAWORTH, INC.

Back in the early 1980s, leaders at Haworth, Inc., the office furniture manufacturer, sought to revitalize their company without benefit of consultants or a wave of downsizings and new hires. Instead, they enrolled all their "members," Haworth's word for employees, in study groups. Using management consultant Richard Schonberger's *Japanese Manufacturing Techniques* as a textbook, everyone from plant managers to assembly line workers absorbed the concept of just-in-time manufacturing, built on run quantities of one, with no inventory. They rigorously analyzed its potential impact on their current mode of operation, and then they went out and redesigned their processes to make it happen.

Today, courses on just-in-time manufacturing are part of the standard educational program for new Haworth factory workers. The study groups still operate, but now they look for ways to get even more innovative in their business design. Bob Milstead, director of manufacturing, says their new culture and competency, which began to shift with the focus on education, is their competitive advantage. "Now," he says, "we are completely immersed in building units of one."

Workers' education is kept current with a corporate weekly newsletter as well as meetings held three or four times a year at which the strategic issues the company faces are discussed. The sessions review what the market is doing and the impact on Haworth. These issues take on particular importance as workers pursue customer and market events.

Milstead says:

I'll tell you, you had better not underestimate the intelligence and the interest of people. For example, at the last member meeting we were talking about our Asian strategy and some of the projects we were working on, and the subject of Hong Kong came up. I couldn't believe the questions that factory members were asking about political things, such as "What's the impact on Haworth when Hong Kong reverts to Chinese rule?" I don't know what it is—cable television or CNN or what—but they are very aware of what's going on in the world.

- ### *Insight:* Embed the strategic purpose.

Before the kinetic transformation can commence, the organization's leaders must set the boundaries within which workers will invent the future. The strategic purpose lays down those boundaries. In Einstein's case, the strategy changed from a focus on filling hospital beds in an acute-care hospital to improving the health of the patient by whatever means possible.

Einstein's leadership team surrounded the workforce with the message of the strategic purpose in every interaction with workers across the organization. And the message was reinforced by briefing sessions, newsletters, bulletin boards, and training courses.

Today, Einstein's leaders know the organization and its offerings will change, adapt, and evolve as workers lead the way. The strategic purpose will be the beacon that workers follow as they recreate the Albert Einstein Healthcare Network over and over again.

- *Insight:* Define the new way to operate.

As we have seen, workers in a kinetic enterprise operate in a brand-new way: They put customers first, take the initiative, cooperate and collaborate with colleagues, and think and act with the entire enterprise in mind. The leadership team must not only define the kinetic model but be the first to show how it plays out day to day.

At Einstein the CEO defined the new way to operate with a set of value statements. Then he insisted that his leadership team begin to live by those values, and he moved out executives who refused to change their old command-and-control work style. He established systems to help every worker understand the values and identify what was needed to live by them.

- *Insight:* Train workers to play any role, anytime.

Kinetic workers are expected to play many roles, from strategist to team leader to project manager, and the organization must invest in programs that prepare workers for those responsibilities. Einstein's kinetic solution was to enable workers themselves to determine the kind of training they needed, while Einstein provided experienced guidance if desired.

Haworth took a more gradualist approach as managers and workers studied and learned together what the experts were saying and what other companies were doing. Training was not used as a vehicle for dragging workers along after the fact, after leaders or outside consultants had already redesigned the business. Instead, leaders helped to get everyone focused on the marketplace and encouraged workers to reinvent themselves so they could reinvent their business.

- *Insight:* **Manage the transfer of control.**

The transformation of top-down change initiatives into events led by the workers themselves is a vital part of the journey toward a kinetic workforce.

But that is not to suggest that management suddenly cedes control of the organization. Control is gradually transferred to workers as they become prepared to exercise it, event by event. The numerous pilot projects initiated by Kentucky provided the perfect environment for that kind of transfer, giving workers invaluable practice dealing with ambiguity, learning on the fly, and implementing real-life solutions.

- *Insight:* **Build vehicles for knowledge transfer.**

To set the kinetic stage, organizations must create a means of capturing and refining the knowledge developed through events and making it available to aid workers in the rest of the enterprise. The chief vehicle chosen for this role by the state of Kentucky, for example, is a Web site that allows workers, citizens living in the state, and workers in other states to check the status and results of workers' projects. In addition, the state set up a newsletter and town hall meetings to keep workers and citizens up to date on the status of the various projects.

- *Insight:* **Allow workers to chart their own course.**

Corporate careers have traditionally been managed by bosses or human resources staff. Kinetic workers take a different tack. They chart their own course event by event, maximizing their learning, building competencies, and opening doors as they go.

Leading companies today are making it crystal clear that workers must take responsibility for their own careers, that the organization will not do the job. But the companies are at pains to make sure workers understand the major factors that affect careers, including workers' comprehension of the dynamics of the marketplace and their implementation of the organization's strategic purpose and boundaries.

Leading companies are encouraging workers to network well beyond the boundaries of their organization so they can keep pace with shifting customer demands and market opportunities—the stuff that kinetic careers are made of. These companies continually allocate massive resources to assessment, training, and education with an eye to preparing workers for the future.

Finally, pioneering organizations are making mentors and coaches available to help workers chart their careers as they move from event to event. But, as you would expect, it is the workers' responsibility to search out and select those coaches.

You may recall our Sarah Brownmiller scenario from chapter 5. She very consciously fashioned her own career by accumulating new learning and competencies as she moved from event to event. And each new challenge, covering a broad range of customer needs and market opportunities, opened doors to even greater career opportunities.

- *Insight:* **Use projects to train for events.**

To become kinetic, organizations need workers who can operate within the new business model—organizing on the fly. The change initiatives that have become so prevalent of late can be perfect practice fields for worker-led, spontaneous events.

In the course of pilot transformation projects in Kentucky, workers practiced spotting opportunities, creating a business case, competing for funds, assembling teams, and interacting with experts from multiple disciplines. At Haworth, workers learned in study groups to walk before they ran; they worked together in new ways and tested and refined ideas before taking them to market. At Einstein, think tanks, experimental process redesign groups, and brainstorming huddles gave workers a chance to work in multidisciplinary teams.

Today's projects—task forces, project teams, ad hoc issues groups—can provide basic training for tomorrow's kinetic transformation.

REWARD FOR SUCCESS

In traditional companies, worker rewards are tied to predefined jobs, to the performance of specific departments or processes, and to moving up the corporate ladder. Workers have to move up a rung to get pay raises.

In a kinetic enterprise, these old approaches simply do not work. Instead, companies compensate workers according to three basic criteria:

1. *Reward enterprise-wide performance.* Kinetic organizations reward workers for contributions to the success of the enterprise as a whole. Microsoft, for example, relies heavily on stock options in lieu of salary to motivate a broad range of workers. Kinko's directly rewards an idea that impacts the performance of the whole company or an individual store. Companies such as Dell and Hewlett-Packard have significant profit-sharing opportunities for all employees. At Deere & Company all workers, including unionized hourly workers, share in a profit-sharing plan based on increases in productivity and quality. Starbucks grants stock options to each employee who works over twenty hours a week, including those serving customers behind the counter in every store, to encourage a sense of ownership among its workers.

2. *Reward behavior, not just results.* To become kinetic, most organizations have to achieve a radical change in the attitudes and behavior of every worker, from the boardroom to the front line. The old command-and-control approaches used by managers are out, as are passive, play-it-safe responses by employees. If everyone is to be a worker, everyone must share responsibility for operating, day in and day out, with the best interests of the organization in mind. Agreed-upon values and

operating principles must be adhered to, because they make spontaneous collaboration and the whole kinetic enterprise possible. But they must be supported by the reward system, or they will fall by the wayside.

In other words, the means are actually more important than the ends. Getting results—even great results—is not enough if it means violating values or principles.

At Southwest, workers who do not appear to exemplify the airline's teamwork values simply do *not* get hired or promoted. At GE, CEO Jack Welch has made it clear that his leadership team must buy into the principles of the boundaryless organization that he believes makes GE a great company, and those whose behavior fails to exemplify that commitment are fired. At Einstein, the degree to which workers' actions reflect shared values determines who will be chosen to manage and lead, and it is part of the formal performance evaluation and feedback process for all workers.

3. *Reward with more than money.* We all recognize in theory that workers can be motivated with psychological rewards and with financial support for favorite projects rather than personal profit. Yet most organizations limit themselves to pay increases. Kinetic organizations do better. At MCI and Aerial Communications we saw companies promoting common goals across the company and publicly recognizing those contributing to their success. At 3M, employees get 15 percent of their time to work on projects of interest to them and can apply for grants of up to $75,000 to carry forward their ideas.

The feelings of pride and achievement that accompany a sense of ownership in an enterprise constitute another significant kind of reward. Kinko's, Southwest, and Starbucks actively promote those feelings. And Thermo Electron carries the idea to its logical conclusion, offering ambitious workers a shot at being CEOs. Corporate recognition, the praise of one's peers —these are the most underused motivational weapons in the business arsenal today.

In this chapter we have dwelled at length on the process of finding and preparing the kinetic workforce so that it can achieve real-time collaboration. We have suggested that infinitely adaptable processes, technologies, and facilities are essential to that goal. In the chapter that follows we offer a tour of the infrastructure that companies should have in place if they are to become truly kinetic.

CHAPTER 8

THE THIRD PATH

DESIGN FOR INSTANT ACTION

How do you pursue the outrageous goals of profitably serving a single customer and acting in zero time without tripping over your infrastructure? You design processes, technology, and facilities for simultaneous, spontaneous work.
Here's how.

THE CONTRAST between traditional and kinetic enterprises is nowhere so stark as in their different takes on infrastructure—the processes, technology, and facilities that support a company's operations.

Traditional organizations build infrastructures primarily to promote productivity and efficiency, with the result that all too often they lock themselves into old ways of doing business. Kinetic enterprises, on the other hand, gear their infrastructures to a pair of outrageous goals. Work designs, communications and computer systems, and even physical plants are designed to serve single customers and to act in zero time.

To achieve those goals, companies must design the following essential elements: protocols for simultaneous work, networks for spontaneous collaboration and learning, information technology for zero-time transactions, process technology to serve single customers, and facilities for adaptability.

DESIGN PROTOCOLS FOR SIMULTANEOUS WORK

The power of the kinetic model resides in its ability to marshal the combined strengths of the workers, physical and intellectual, to immediately pursue and complete events. But that kind of spontaneous action is impossible in traditional companies governed by traditional work rules, with their linear, step-by-step organization of tasks. In place of the old work rules, kinetic enterprises create shared protocols that enable workers to simultaneously address a challenge—shifting roles, shifting sequence, and shifting tasks—all the while adhering to well-understood boundaries and principles.

The hospital emergency room provides a model of the kinetic design for simultaneous work in action. Emergency room residents are trained and practiced in the team-oriented protocols that make it possible to cope with each patient's particular set of injuries and needs. When a patient arrives, the first resident or nurse on the scene takes charge and executes lifesaving procedures. When a physician appears, he or she takes charge, and the resident or nurse shifts to a supporting role, setting up life support machines and calling out readings of the patient's vital signs. As more medical staff join in, the various members of the team smoothly shift roles again and again to serve the common purpose.

In the kinetic enterprise, that same flexibility and freedom from ironclad work rules prevails. Multidisciplinary teams meet in person and in cyberspace to plan and execute events, deciding what they must do, how they must do it, and which members are best qualified or best positioned to take on which assignments. Individuals immediately set about their tasks. The whole process happens at once, simultaneously, in real time.

The Boeing Company and a number of health care companies are setting the pace for the application of technology and team protocols for simultaneous work.

THE BOEING COMPANY

The Boeing 777 was what people in the aircraft business call a clean-sheet plane—one started from scratch in terms of materials, electronics, navigation, and even cabin design. It provided the company with an occasion to totally rethink its design process, and it led to the introduction of a technology that enabled the entire design team—customers, manufacturers, engineers, and suppliers—to operate in a virtual environment while performing massive simultaneous work.

Earlier planes had relied on a series of mock-ups, a process that began with computer-aided drawings of an airliner's one hundred thousand designed parts. The drawings were used to make parts made of plywood and foam that became the so-called Stage-1 mock-up. Inevitably, the parts produced by thousands of different designers did not fit together. When two pieces overlapped, they were said to "interfere."

Some corrections were reflected in the Stage-2 mock-up, some metal parts were added, and it began to address complicated issues of routing wiring and tubing. It was followed by the Stage-3 mock-up, in which every component of the airplane was constructed by hand according to engineering drawings, incorporating discoveries and changes made during the first two stages. Finally, the airliner was put into production.

In Karl Sabbagh's *Twenty-First Century Jet,* Dick Johnson, one of Boeing's top engineers, describes the process:

> You have 5,000 engineers designing the airplane. It's very difficult for those engineers to coordinate with two-dimensional pieces of paper, or for a designer who is designing an air-conditioning duct to walk over to somebody who is in Structures and say, "Now, here's my duct—how does it match up with your structure?" Very difficult with two-dimensional pictures. We ended up using the mock-up and, quite honestly, also using the final assembly line to finish up the integration. And it's very costly. You end up with an airplane that's very difficult to build. The first time that parts come together is on that assembly line. And they don't fit.

The computer-aided design system Boeing implemented just prior to the 777 project did allow engineers to see their individual parts in three dimensions, a major breakthrough from a decade before, but it could not show how the parts fit into the design of the entire aircraft. And it could do nothing about another problem that had traditionally plagued aircraft production: the turf consciousness of the various disciplines engaged in the enterprise. It inevitably resulted in various degrees of turmoil and inefficiency.

Engineers tend to be self-sufficient, independent types. They want to be given a problem and then left alone to solve it. So when parts from one engineer came together with parts from other engineers in the mock-ups, the parts overlapped. Interference.

The problem was compounded by the arm's length relationship between engineers and the manufacturing staff. After engineering designed a part, the manufacturing department would design a production tool that could make the part in quantity. Some of these tools were immense. The two-hundred-foot-long "ASAT" tool filled ninety trucks with its parts. But in many cases the complexity and cost of producing such tools could have been reduced by collaboration between engineering and manufacturing while the parts were being designed.

Determined to eliminate these problems, Boeing devised a database called EPIC, for Electronic Preassembly in the Computer. Its first assignment was the 777. Engineers still designed their parts on computer as they had done before, but now they could simultaneously see exactly how the parts fit together in the aircraft. If an interference showed up, one designer could immediately contact the other and resolve the problem rather than discovering the misfit months later on the assembly floor.

Simultaneous work radically reduced coordination problems. Consider the computer check of a single three-dimensional assembly of a wing flap: The computer made more than 200,000 checks and found 251 interferences. In each instance the designers of the respective components and their neighbors met in person or electronically as ad hoc, real-time teams to decide who was to redesign which part, taking into account the effects any change might have on the strength of the assembly as a whole.

Other key players in the process, from airframe component manufacturers in Japan to engine makers in America and the United Kingdom, also had access to cyberspace design. With real-time access to the most current parts design, manufacturers could work with engineers to design parts that were easier and cheaper to produce.

A number of potential mistakes were avoided by the participation of customers in the simultaneous work. In one case a customer noticed that the planned height of the 777's fueling panel put it substantially above the level of the fuel stands used by airlines. At that height, customers for the new aircraft would have been unable to refuel it.

HEALTH CARE COMPANIES

The way it's always been, ambulance drivers are chartered to stabilize patients until they arrive at the hospital and can be seen by emergency room personnel who then decide on what treatment should be given and what medical experts, if any, should be called in on the case. That linear process sometimes results in patients dying before they get into the right medical hands.

In the following scenarios we show how that linear approach can be turned into simultaneous work with the help of new technology, a mobile infrastructure, and a real-time approach. In fact, many of the devices mentioned are now being tested in the field.

Event Number 1: Siren wailing, an ambulance draws up to an accident scene. The ambulance attendant wears a telemedicine camera attached to his helmet, beaming an image of the injured driver to the emergency room physician back at the hospital. Ambulance attendant and physician agree that the patient can be transported to the hospital. En route, the attendant hooks up an IV and monitors the patient's vital signs, which are transmitted to the physician. When the patient is rolled into the emergency room, the staff is ready to administer the right treatment, immediately.

Event Number 2: The driver at the accident scene is seriously injured. The ambulance attendant hesitates to move her, and the emergency room physician, scanning the scene via the telemedicine camera, agrees. The physician guides the attendant in applying specific lifesaving procedures—right at the accident site. When the patient is stabilized, she is transported to the hospital.

Event Number 3: The driver is in critical condition. The ambulance attendant and the emergency room physician agree to call a special telemedicine unit to the scene. A surgeon is alerted and reports to the hospital operating room. There, guided by interactive video, he manipulates a robot at the accident scene to perform emergency surgery on the injured driver. The patient is stabilized and then transported to the hospital.

• *Insight:* **Create team protocols for simultaneous work.**

The members of a kinetic team are all experts in their own right, familiar with the ideas and practices of their disciplines, from the latest technical developments to the relevant government regulations. From these building blocks, the team designs the right approach for each situation.

Sometimes the challenge is totally fresh, never before encountered, and each team member digs deep to come up with alternative approaches on the way to a new solution. Often, the actual work performed by team members is familiar, but the manner in which the work is combined and sequenced is new and different for each and every customer.

Whatever the particular solution, it must be arrived at rapidly and implemented immediately, on the fly. As in the emergency room, there is no time to wait to round up support for a particular action within the upper reaches of the organization. There is no time for extended debate when your suggestion is overruled. Team members understand that they operate under a set of guidelines, that decisions must be made quickly if the system is to succeed, and they accept the uncertainties and risks that entails. They also understand that by persevering they constantly improve and evolve their simultaneous work skills.

- *Insight:* **Provide the technology for virtual teamwork.**

Specialized technology—such as the EPIC design database at Boeing and the interactive video system for medical emergency treatment—makes it possible for teams to meet in a virtual workspace to develop products and deliver personalized service. Thus the linear processes of traditional companies can be collapsed into simultaneous work, eliminating the errors and delays that have plagued corporations for generations.

DESIGN NETWORKS FOR SPONTANEOUS COLLABORATION AND LEARNING

If workers are to operate simultaneously, they must be able to spontaneously communicate with, partner with, and learn from coworkers, leaders, suppliers, and customers. They must be plugged into networks, personal and technological, that make it possible for everyone to learn from the experience of everyone else, quickly tapping the products, services, and competencies they need to satisfy a unique customer demand or to exploit a new market opportunity.

When it comes to networks, Kaiser Permanente and eight hundred Taiwanese-American companies set the pace.

KAISER PERMANENTE

Consider Kaiser Permanente's corporate office; its staff of four hundred is based at their headquarters in Oakland, California, and at two other regional sites. Until 1995 the office operated like most functional organizations. Each of the twenty departments had its own network, electronic mail system, brands of PCs, and favorite PC software, so that electronic mail, computer information, and PC files could not be shared by departments or workers.

In 1995, Kaiser decided to create a single communications, information, and knowledge network for the corporate office that could be expanded over time to support Kaiser's enterprise. The company believed that networked workers—operating with up-to-date information, accessing the organization's knowledge, and collaborating by way of electronic mail—could vastly improve their learning skills and agility.

Dr. David Lawrence, the CEO, supported the campaign to convince employees of the need for the overhaul. He also let his top people know that no one was too important, too old, or too busy to learn the new technology. That included executives who had been with Kaiser for forty years and relied on their secretaries to download daily e-mails and create word-processing documents, spreadsheets, and presentations. It also included Dr. Lawrence himself. He quickly became computer literate, managing his own schedule electronically and taking advantage of frequent long flights to prepare updates on the company to be published via Lotus Notes on the Kaiser network.

Long before the new personal computers were brought in, Kaiser offered workers a variety of training and support options so they could update their skills. When the equipment arrived in any given department, support people actually outnumbered employees. What's more, in replacing its old local area networks

(LANs) with a single network accessible by every worker, Kaiser made sure that workers' new computers were set up exactly as their old ones had been. File names and directory structures remained intact, and the files in each computer were already converted to the new software programs.

Every corporate office employee received a personal computer, 30 percent of which were laptops. "We spend a lot of time serving the many Kaiser Permanente divisions around the country, so our travel schedule is extensive," says Chris Van Noy, director of administrative services and executive assistant to Dr. Lawrence. "We really have to be able to spontaneously communicate and interact with 'anyone, anytime, anywhere.' "

Anytime, anywhere can mean 2:00 A.M. in a hotel room or 10:00 Saturday morning in an employee's backyard. Hank Russell, manager of information technology systems and services, no longer feels the need to go to the office on weekends. "Now I do work from my deck. I can either work off-line if I'm just creating things, or if I need to communicate, I can log in." And the laptop is there when a brainstorm strikes. "It's wonderful to have the ability to immediately communicate a thought or idea when it comes into your head," Van Noy says. "That speaks to efficiency, but it also allows you to be more creative."

New employees are quickly wired. By noon of a new hire's first day of work, an electronic purchase order has been transmitted to Entex, Kaiser's technology partner. Within twenty-four hours the computer arrives from Entex, already configured to Kaiser standards. Within forty-eight hours the worker receives her network ID and Lotus Notes account, and is listed in all the electronic directories.

Lotus Notes serves as the great two-way communicator, making data immediately available and allowing workers to share ideas and information in real time. A presentation that would once have been printed to the tune of 350 copies and distributed through interoffice mail can now be instantly transmitted over the network.

Workers and hundreds of affiliated medical professionals can also access a Lotus Notes database to share best practices and knowledge. A database called Accumulated Organization Knowledge contains thousands of abstracts of research papers written by Kaiser medical professionals. Another database shares best practices. For example, if someone in Washington, D.C., discovers a surgical operation that can be done better or faster, it can be instantly shared with doctors as far away as Hawaii. The newest knowledge base contains protocols and manuals on how to care for patients from different cultures. When a native of Tonga moves into Atlanta, for example, her new physician can learn about that nation's culture and medical traditions from knowledge-base entries based on the experiences of physicians in south San Francisco, which has a large Tongan population.

The wiring of Kaiser's workers has spurred a productivity increase far beyond the 2 percent to 3 percent predicted by the business office when it originally argued for installing the new technology. The flexibility as to when and where one can work is such that even Dr. Lawrence acknowledges "the challenge is knowing when to unplug."

EIGHT HUNDRED TAIWANESE-AMERICAN COMPANIES

Some networks are held together by more than technology. In the southern California computer industry, 800 Taiwanese-American companies, bound by trust and teamwork resulting from common values and continuous collaboration, have developed a resource network and a spontaneous partnering capacity that competitors cannot match.

The participants range from tiny ten-person start-ups to companies like ViewSonic, which has 350 employees in seven countries. Instead of the usual complex and time-consuming contractual arrangements, the members of the network become partners on one's word to satisfy a single customer's need. Their close physical proximity also helps. Hundreds of computer companies are located within a half-hour drive of each other.

Here's how a typical customer event might work: A retailer wants to market a state-of-the-art personal computer under its own brand name. The retailer approaches one of the eight hundred companies—a maker of motherboards, the brains of the personal computer. The motherboard firm then teams with a California company that manufactures CD-ROM drives in Taiwan, a keyboard dealer who can import a new ergonomic model, and a dozen other suppliers of PC parts.

When a brand-new part is needed, the companies network with design firms in Silicon Valley and overseas Taiwan manufacturers to design and manufacture the part. Eventually, the motherboard company assembles and delivers the private label computer line to its customer.

The bond in common values that holds this network together and gives it such flexibility and speed of response is becoming a familiar element of the competitive landscape as globalization reaches out to cultures around the world.

- *Insight:* **Build an enterprise-wide network.**

There is nothing simple about wiring an enterprise for collaboration and learning. That's why organizations such as Kaiser are picking a place in the enterprise to pilot the new approach. It demands that separate systems dedicated to departments or processes must yield to standard PCs, standard PC software, and standard services such as e-mail and Lotus Notes.

As Kaiser's Lawrence demonstrated, the transformation requires leaders who are both cheerleaders and role models. Workers must be trained and supported. A whole new culture of collaboration and learning across departmental borders and geographic boundaries must be set in place.

- *Insight:* **Partner on the fly.**

Networks for spontaneous collaboration don't always require technology, although it helps. As illustrated by the eight hundred Taiwanese-American companies, strong bonds can be developed based on a shared understanding of how companies become partners on the spot. In fact, a network of prequalified partner companies, bound by a clear set of rules for collaboration, can be as strong as any wired by technology.

DESIGN INFORMATION TECHNOLOGY
TO DELIVER IN ZERO TIME

In the kinetic enterprise, employees are expected to work and learn simultaneously in order to execute events in as close to zero time as possible. To achieve that goal, they must be able to access accurate, up-to-the-second information when, where, and how they want it. And once they have initiated a customer event, they must have immediate execution; they cannot wait for batch computer programs to grind out executions overnight.

AMAZON.COM

The prototype of the zero-time customer event is available on the Internet twenty-four hours a day, every day of the year, at Amazon.com. The site lists an amazing 1.1 million of the 1.5 million English-language books in print. In a *Fast Company* article, Jeff Bezos, founder and CEO, says, "There's no way you can build a store to handle 1.1 million titles, and you can't offer our selection in a catalog. If you printed the Amazon.com catalog, it would be the size of fourteen New York City phone books." And that doesn't include the million out-of-print books on Amazon.com's inventory list.

The Web site allows customers to initiate their own transactions by placing an order online. Customers can also rearrange the shelves to their own liking, listing the kinds of books they want to read; if it's mysteries, for example, Amazon.com will have a list of the hottest new whodunits ready and waiting for the customer's next visit. Customers can be "visible" or "invisible," as they choose, when they enter one or another section of the virtual bookstore. If visible, they can ask other customers: "Read any good books lately?"

When an order is placed, Amazon.com immediately searches available inventories, its own and those of other distributors. When the book is located, a shipping order is issued, the customer's credit card is debited, the books are posted, and a confirming e-mail message is sent to the customer with a shipping number. Transaction complete.

PHARMACEUTICAL, INC.

To make decisions and to make corrections on the spot, workers must have immediate access to the right information, and it must be presented in a form they can quickly and easily comprehend.

Five years ago the CFO of a privately held pharmaceutical firm was taking the organization public. He knew that once the organization came under the scrutiny of stockholders, he and his workers would need tighter control over the enterprise.

Everyone received monthly reports on the revenues generated by the company's twenty product lines, but those reports failed to provide any insight into the performance of the company's twenty thousand individual products. So the CFO sought out his director of technology and asked for a new computer system that would track individual products instead of just product lines.

The technology director refused, in a manner of speaking. He agreed to design a new system, but he insisted that it be not only for tracking individual products. Indeed, the system he built also provided revenue summaries and detailed order information in any format the inquirer chose—by product, by product line, by sales representative, by geographic territory, by customer, by order size, and more. To help everyone spot problems and opportunities quickly, the information was updated with each order received and made available to everyone in the company on a daily basis.

When the company went public, workers aggressively monitored and managed the performance of the company's twenty thousand products. But that wasn't the news. Within two years management bought back the company, decided to expand globally, and needed detailed product sales information by country. The news was that the computer system delivered the new information with a single click of a mouse.

- *Insight:* **Handle customer transactions one at a time.**

In most organizations, computer systems are designed to process transactions in batches. Once a week or so, thousands of invoices are calculated, printed, and mailed. Once a month the accounting books are reconciled and closed. Sometime after that, management reports are updated with the latest sales, revenue, and cost information.

In a kinetic organization each customer transaction is handled to completion instantly—the way Amazon.com does it.

The instant an order is received, the customer's bank account is charged or the invoice is calculated and an image stored electronically, ready for printing when needed. The accounting books are electronically updated with the customer's transaction. Management information is also updated with the single customer order.

With this approach the performance of the enterprise can be viewed at any time. The manager's information is updated order by order like a stock market ticker tape. The CFO's month-end financial statements are simply printouts of the exact status of the enterprise at specific points in time.

To be kinetic, companies must design systems that allow everyone in the enterprise to act on a single customer request—at once.

- *Insight:* **Design applications that put workers in charge.**

In traditional organizations, programmers code computer applications with predefined policies, procedures, controls, and reporting formats. In a kinetic enterprise, new computer tools give workers maximum flexibility without depending on MIS for reprogramming.

In our pharmaceutical company example, databases and PC software allow workers to access, review, and analyze information any way they choose. With this information, workers can answer customer questions and make decisions—*now.*

DESIGN PROCESS TECHNOLOGY TO SERVE SINGLE CUSTOMERS

In a mass-market world, process technology has but a single major goal: maximize production runs to minimize unit costs. That works fine as long as the public remains content with a limited number of product options. But time has run out on the mass market. Business is being forced to respond to individual customer demands. And that means process technology must take on a new mission. It must make it possible for organizations to serve single customers, responding to an infinite number of customer needs with split-second speed and flexibility.

ANDERSEN WINDOWS

A $1 billion, privately held window manufacturer based in Bayport, Minnesota, Andersen decided in 1992 to let customers design their own windows. At that time, as Mike Tremblay, manager of business systems, puts it, according to a *Fortune* article, the market "kept asking for more and more unique things. People didn't want their windows to look like their neighbor's windows, or anyone else's in the world, for that matter." So Andersen installed virtual-design software at 650 of its dealers around the United States.

It was a dramatic departure for the company, which began producing windows on an assembly line in 1904. Over the years the company had tried to keep up with customer demands by adding more and more options to its catalog. Eventually it got to the point where it could take hours to work up a price quote that might be fifteen pages long. And to satisfy complicated demands—from a customer seeking arched windows, for example—the salesperson had to have a working knowledge of geometry to make up the order. Not surprisingly, the ever-more-complicated process took its toll on service: From 1985 to 1991, a period when product offerings rose from twenty-eight thousand to eighty-six thousand, the number of order discrepancies doubled.

The software package that Andersen chose to champion with its retailers and distributors runs on a personal computer and sells for about $4,000. Salespeople can now help customers add, change, and strip away features until they have designed on the computer screen the windows they want. Then the software checks the window specifications for structural soundness and generates a price quote. Every order receives a unique identification number at the factory and can be tracked from assembly line to shipping bay in real time using bar code technology.

The number of errors has plummeted. What's more, retailers and their employees no longer have to possess advanced mathematical knowledge and design skills in order to market Andersen Windows.

Andersen dealer David Steele, who, as president of the Window Gallery, operates three locations in the Southeast, says the new system enables him to produce a window to fit a customer's specifications five times faster, and it has been a major factor in tripling his sales of Andersen products in the past five years.

The system has effectively made Steele and other retailers part of Andersen Windows' virtual, instant-action enterprise.

HAWORTH, INC.

In the old days at Haworth, production was a simple affair. The factory cut wooden desktops to dozens of standard sizes, and they were warehoused along with inventories of different-colored laminates and edge trims. Workers assembled a customer's order by drawing from the desktops, laminates, and edge colors piled in the warehouse.

The whole operation depended on management's ability to predict accurately what kind of furniture its corporate customers would order. But as the business environment changed, Haworth recognized that its crystal ball was clouded. "You can imagine all the different veneer woods, stains, finishes, fabrics, colors, sizes, and shapes that furniture can come in," says Bob Milstead, the director of manufacturing. "You can never guess what a customer is going to want."

As noted in the previous chapter, Haworth adopted the Japanese production approach as its model and moved toward a system based on run quantities of one and just-in-time supply. Today, the company can design desktops and other pieces in virtually any size or shape.

This is how it happens: Haworth dealers determine the design of the furniture with the customer and electronically send in the order, which goes directly into the company's enterprise-wide computer system. The order for the appropriate pieces of raw wood or blank steel is issued, and the design is downloaded right to the machine on the factory floor that cuts the pattern. It is virtually instantaneous, Milstead says. "We don't even have to touch it."

The production process is continuous until the finished furniture is in a box and on a truck. All customization—such as grommet holes to accommodate telephone and power cables—is handled automatically by computerized machinery. The speed of the entire operation is remarkable. "It takes about one day to run the MRP [materials requirement planning] systems and to get the order down to the factory floor," says Milstead. "Then it's three days to put the order through the factories, and a day to get it on a truck and ship it. So it's a five-day process from the time we receive an order until it can be shipped, and that goes for anything from a few chairs to a $20 million order."

For nervous customers, that schedule takes some getting used to. Typically, they place an order six weeks before they need to furnish, say, a new office building, and a week later they call to see if Haworth has started manufacturing it yet. Haworth workers have to explain that the order won't actually arrive at the factory until five days before shipment.

SOLUTIA

Not so long ago, Solutia's chemical plant in Pensacola, Florida, operated twenty-four hours a day, seven days a week, spinning out continuous strands of a variety of fibers. Fiber products were then warehoused in anticipation of customer orders. One day the plant might produce nylon fibers that a customer manufacturer would weave into a carpet. Another day it might turn out industrial nylon products used in heavy-duty tires.

Robert Barrett, worldwide operations and financial project director, explains Solutia's old approach: "The goal was maintaining long, continuous runs and minimizing changeovers. Unfortunately, manufacturing excellence does not always provide what customers want. As customers increasingly demanded something different—and wanted it fast—business became a series of mini-crises."

A customer would call a Solutia service representative with an order. The representative would call the plant to make sure the product ordered was in inventory. If it was not, the representative would get a production planner on the telephone to figure out when the product could be made. The production planner lacked the authority to modify the production plan because that would require a schedule break. He had to consult with a business manager or the production superintendent.

This procedure was costly in terms of workers' time—answers might be forthcoming in a half hour or a few days—and it did nothing for the customer's frame of mind. When all was said and done, it often turned out that delivery had to be delayed.

Things are very different these days. Solutia's new systems and business practices have transformed the plant's operation. Now customers can enter orders twenty-four hours a day, direct from their computers to Solutia's. Those orders literally schedule production at the plant.

That means Solutia's ability to deliver is tied directly to how well its customers plan and schedule their own production.

Because of this electronic umbilical cord, the manufacturer-customer can see when its Solutia order is going to be delivered, when its invoice will go out, and how much it will be billed. Customers are so intimately wired to Solutia that they begin to view the fiber plant as if it were their own.

Barrett explains what the new strategy offers customers: "If I give you access to my plant, give you the ability to control it —virtually control it—I'll share my cost savings with you, my customer. If we work together to get costs out of the supply chain, I'll pass my savings on to you."

The technological change at the Solutia plant has been matched by a cultural change that reaches to every corner of the operation. Workers no longer think of their role as "just making batch chemicals." They no longer measure their personal success by how well they do their own jobs or how much chemical product they produce on a given day. At the end of a shift, workers—from the operator on the floor to the CFO—receive information on the cost and quality of fiber turned out for each customer order. That is how they now measure their success, and they use that information to look for new ways to do their work better for each customer order.

- *Insight:* **Eliminate order entry.**

As Andersen Windows learned to its delight, new technology —virtual-design software, in its case—can transform complex, custom orders into simple transactions. Errors and delays in creating and submitting the orders were drastically trimmed. By wiring dealers to the kinetic enterprise, every party to the transaction, including the factory and its suppliers, can work simultaneously to meet a single customer's need.

- *Insight:* **Produce units of one.**

In a kinetic corporation, process technologies are designed to produce units of one economically. Our examples make the case. At Haworth the new approach eliminated inventory and delays while satisfying the personal needs of each and every customer.

Solutia carried the units-of-one principle a step further, designing its operations and systems to allow customers' computers to schedule the Solutia plant.

Technological innovation has spread the units-of-one concept far and wide. At R. R. Donnelley & Sons Company, for example, the high cost of setting up its printing presses always had to be offset by a high-volume run, so the company could not afford to print small runs of books. The trouble was, customer demand for the small runs was growing mightily. A few years ago Donnelley found the solution: building a new printing plant that could run off text stored in digital form, which can be economically printed in any quantity, whether it be a million or one.

- *Insight:* **Eliminate inventory.**

To produce units of one economically, companies must eliminate inventory. Suppliers must deliver materials just in time to match the day's production plans for specific customer orders.

And that requires a new and more intimate relationship with suppliers than most organizations now maintain. As Haworth does it, suppliers are wired to the enterprise, privy to the inner operations of their customers, working simultaneously with dealers and factory to meet a single customer's need.

DESIGN FACILITIES FOR ADAPTABILITY

If workers are to be allowed to act simultaneously and spontaneously, the facilities in which they work must be built to flex, not built to last. When you cannot predict the future, your factory or supermarket or design studio must be capable of responding to the infinite variety of challenges tossed your way by customers, partners, and competitors.

CITYTV

Moses Znaimer has a vision for the television studio of the future, and he's seeing it taking shape today: His Toronto-based Citytv is housed in a 160,000-square-foot studio that has no interior walls, no fixed work schedules, and, best of all, no pre-programmed pablum from promoters of national broadcasting systems. As Znaimer sees it, nothing could be worse for television than the attitude that programming anywhere should look like programming everywhere. The philosophy of sameness may be fine for airport construction, strip malls, and french fries, but not for television.

Znaimer argues that the thousand or so TV stations located

from Seattle to Singapore are, after all, pretty much the same: Turn on a TV in Paris and you'll probably find a talk show or a sitcom that looks like its counterpart in London.

That's why Znaimer has worked to make Citytv unique and flexible: To accomplish that feat, he has broken down the walls inside the five-story office building on Queen Street West in Toronto, outfitted twenty-five news cruisers and two trucks capable of transmitting "live action" reports from anywhere in the surrounding area, and installed some one hundred traffic and weather "eyes," remote-control cameras that never miss a beat of the city's pulse.

Znaimer's strategy is to make Citytv absolutely local, to bring the outside inside, and to invite the people of Toronto to be the programmers and actors of their own shows. For example, the downtown studio facility is laid out as if in a "streetwise" pattern, making it difficult sometimes to distinguish what goes on inside from what's happening on the outside. For a music-awards show, thousands of fans gather outside the studio to make this a media event without bounds and without walls. Viewers—frequently referred to as "participants"—use the popular QuickTally, a computerized poll that counts twenty thousand calls and e-mails per hour, to offer their opinions on any program or newsworthy item that appears on the local broadcast. The upshot is that Citytv is both entertaining and interactive, a combination that sets it apart from the run-of-the-mill TV stations that grind viewers into mental mush.

Citytv now employs more than two hundred people, up from the eighty or so who joined Znaimer when he started the station back in 1972. People work all sorts of hours, often burning the midnight oil, giving the notion of flextime a significance that it rarely gets in ordinary workplaces. Indeed, the motto for Citytv might be "Ideas don't sleep, so why should we?"

VOLKSWAGEN

At the experimental $300 million Volkswagen plant in Resende, Brazil, workers from seven companies are building new VW trucks. In fact, the whole production line is run from start to finish by these "partner" companies, each simultaneously assembling and installing components. Volkswagen provides the empty building, and VW inspectors maintain quality control on the assembly line. Otherwise, in this Alice in Wonderland of a plant, the seven partners do it all, bringing their latest equipment and expertise to bear on their joint project.

The factory floor is crisscrossed with dozens of yellow painted lines, each demarcating a separate corporate territory. In one area you'll find Rockwell do Brasil, a subsidiary of the United States–based maker of brakes and suspension systems. In another, is VDO do Brasil, a subsidiary of a German firm that makes instrument panels. Each company is responsible for delivering its supplies according to a just-in-time schedule.

The facility allows Volkswagen to capitalize quickly on its partners' innovations. And because its partners have a direct stake in the production process, they have a built-in incentive to continually improve their performance.

- *Insight:* **Build for adaptability, not just flexibility.**

In both of our examples, the companies started from scratch and with the intention of making their facilities fully adaptable.

Instead of putting together a traditional TV studio that included a few flexible options, Citytv began with an empty building and put in resources that workers could access to spontaneously design and produce one-of-a-kind TV broadcasts.

VW's building was empty, too, and the company arranged for it to be filled by a truck production line operated by its seven supplier-partners. In this way the facility was made totally adaptable to the improvements in equipment, skills, and processes developed by any one of its partners.

In this chapter we discussed some of the infrastructure designs favored by kinetic enterprises in their pursuit of the twin outrageous goals of serving single customers and acting in zero time. In the next chapter we show how these companies prepare their workers to take on customer events.

CHAPTER 9

THE FOURTH PATH

IGNITE CUSTOMER EVENTS

While competitors are crushed by fragmenting markets, kinetic pioneers let customers design their own sales relationship, products, and services.
Here's how.

CUSTOMER events may vary dramatically by company and industry, but they share a common goal: They respond to the particular demands of individual customers. They do it profitably. They do it now. In this chapter we show how organizations prepare for customer events. The dynamic design they put into place enables the organization to adapt to and evolve with each customer they serve.

Like its counterparts in the natural world, the kinetic corporation is built on an evolutionary principle. Since customer loyalty, brand loyalty, must be earned again and again with every transaction, the corporation must learn from each event and possess the flexibility to apply that learning to the next one. As we have pointed out before, the decision to adopt this new basis of competition is not optional. It is essential for corporate survival.

Kinetic enterprises ignite customer events so customers can design their own relationships, create personalized products and services, invent wholly new products and services, and design total solutions.

LET CUSTOMERS DESIGN RELATIONSHIPS

In the old mass-market world, a company selected specific distribution channels to serve specific kinds of customers. In a world of events, companies profit from customer relationships perfectly matched to each customer's needs as defined by the customer.

One customer, for example, might want to join a managed-care organization because of its fitness programs and insists that he be called about every new seminar on nutrition or stress management. Another customer might want the organization to provide nothing more than emergency and routine medical treatment and demands that she be left off all mailing and phone lists. The kinetic organization can accommodate both customer relationships.

How are businesses like the Prudential Insurance Company and a chemical concern we call Pilot Chemicals setting the pace and letting customers design their own relationships? They are opening all channels to all customers, making all of the resources of the enterprise available to a single customer, creating corporate memory, making everyone a customer advocate, and letting those customer advocates manage resources.

THE PRUDENTIAL INSURANCE COMPANY

For years Mark Grier, chief financial officer of Prudential, has championed the delivery of products to the marketplace in ways customers want to buy them. "The financial services company that figures out how to do this will win big," he says. The problem: Customers come in many different varieties. Some want plain vanilla term insurance, while others have very complex financial and insurance needs. Some will study every conceivable product option until the cows come home, while others, trusting souls, are eager to throw themselves on the mercy of the nearest salesperson.

Michael Hines, Prudential's vice president of marketing and communications, speaks of the need for "multiple channels" for the same product: a branch office for you to visit, for example, or a salesperson to visit you in your home or office; a chance for you to conduct all your business over the telephone, either with a person or an interactive system, or to handle your own financial transactions on the Internet. Hines's mission? "To provide all products to all channels, everywhere." Why? "To make doing business with us effortless on the customer's part."

Stand-alone units of a company can no longer sell just their own products. Customers must have the ability to access an organization's complete range of products and services through whatever relationship format they choose. At the same time, to better foster that relationship, customer advocates need to have access to a record of all their customers' experiences with every part of the company.

Although both Grier and Hines admit that realizing their vision is a long way off, Prudential is starting now with an experiment called "The One Prudential Market Test."

In Minneapolis, Richmond, and Phoenix, Prudential is testing ways to let customers buy into any and all of its portfolio of services. In each city the company has assigned real estate experts, financial experts, and insurance experts to a single Prudential office. And they operate very differently from your typical brokers and agents.

In today's information age, says Mark Grier, traditional sales relationships no longer work. "Formerly, the value of supplying data to clients was extremely high because financial advisors and insurance agents were the only source for data. Now you can go online. You can buy *Money* magazine or *Barron's*. You can get data everywhere."

Grier has spotted new relationship opportunities made possible by the information glut: "Look at the number of articles in *The Wall Street Journal* over the past twelve months about people trying to wrestle with the fact that they know so much, but they end up not knowing anything. While data has become a lot cheaper, advice has become more valuable because consumers can't sort it all out."

The shift he is championing—from providing data to giving expert advice—requires a new kind of customer advocate. The advocate is a person or team capable of analyzing clients' needs and creating solutions by mixing and matching a variety of products and services. That's what's happening in the One Prudential Market Test.

The Prudential vision does not take customers' constancy for granted. The company understands that relationship needs and tastes will vary among customers and that each individual's needs and tastes can change from one day or hour to the next. The kinetic enterprise must be prepared for such variety and shifts.

To that end, Prudential is piloting its single database, which consolidates information about a customer's experience with any division of the company. Eventually that information—what and how customers have bought from such diverse areas as financial services, health care, real estate, and insurance—will be made available throughout the organization. With that data, customer advocates will be far better equipped to meet unpredictable demands.

PILOT CHEMICALS

The chemical company we call Pilot had been quietly and steadily selling products to a *Fortune* 500 manufacturing company for years. Then one day the Pilot sales representative called on the client company's vice president of manufacturing and was hit with a totally unexpected list of demands:

1. Quarterly briefings from technical experts on Pilot's latest products and research. The vice president wanted to keep his staff current and positioned to take advantage of research breakthroughs.

2. A semiannual update on his organization's purchasing across all of Pilot's thirty-two divisions. He wanted to orchestrate a broad business partnership with Pilot that would include worldwide discounts for his company on chemical products.

3. Internet access to real-time product announcements and product information—but only those products that complied with his engineering division's specifications.

4. A Pilot global account team to help make sure all divisions of the customer's organization purchased environmentally sensitive products.

The Pilot sales representative, shifting into customer advocate mode, calmly agreed to all of the customer's demands. He knew that the manufacturer's business was too important to lose, and, anyway, Pilot had been organized to cope with just this kind of unpredictable challenge.

The sales representative returned to the office and recruited an international account team by e-mail, sending each member an electronic copy of the customer's relationship plan. Later, in a conference call, the members of the team devised an overall strategy to cope with the new demands that ensured a healthy profit for Pilot.

The sales representative also set up an Internet home page for the customer and announced its availability in an e-mail to the manufacturing vice president. The vice president immediately forwarded the e-mail to his worldwide staff. Finally, the representative scheduled R&D leaders for the first quarterly briefing and set in motion the mechanism for the semiannual update.

- *Insight:* **Open all channels to all customers.**

In an environment where customers call the shots, they must be given a say over every aspect of their interactions with the company. That means companies will have to abandon their strategy of dedicating one distribution channel or business format to one set of products and one kind of customer—say, high-end stores for upscale customers and Internet purchasing for customers who want self-service and a low price. The winning strategy: Allow customers to determine what form interactions will take, be it in person, by telephone, or over the Internet. Then, as the Prudential example suggests, enable them to access a complete range of products and services through any specific channel, whether it be a local branch office, a sales rep who visits the home or office, a twenty-four-hour telephone hotline, or a Web site. And, finally, make it possible for them to switch from one channel to the next on any given day.

- *Insight:* **Make all the resources of the enterprise accessible to a single customer.**

Neither consumers nor corporate customers are willing to settle for the old-style relationships in which companies sell standard products and services, and customers buy from ads, brochures, and price sheets. Today's consumers want access to research information, to educational information and workshops, to personal advisors, and to other customers. As the Pilot Chemicals example indicates, corporate customers want access to proprietary knowledge and backroom experts, and they want client companies (and their workers) to act as part of their own virtual enterprise.

- *Insight:* **Create corporate memory.**

If a customer defines her own relationship, everyone in the organization must know the customer's preferences and deliver them. For example, one consumer may want to receive educational and promotional material in the mail, while another does not. As suggested in the Pilot Chemicals example, one corporate customer may require that his staff buy specific types of products. Another corporate customer may allow its workers to buy any available product.

For workers to deliver, companies must create a single data repository for customer preferences and history; this is no easy task since many *Fortune* 500 companies have dozens or hundreds of computer systems, each containing some form of customer information. A single data repository is designed to track customers' relationships regardless of the distribution channels they access and the divisions or partners who supply the individual products or services.

At the same time, the kinetic organization's systems are designed to let customers call the shots: Web sites are capable of being tailored for a single customer. Billing systems are designed to track costs, and produce invoices as specified by the customer. Direct-mail systems send promotional material only to those customers who want it. Workers have access to databases and systems in which customers' preferences are recorded and met.

- *Insight:* **Make everyone a customer advocate.**

Kinetic corporations are built on the premise that everyone from the CEO to the drill press operator to, as in our Pilot Chemicals example, the sales representative will be ready, willing, and able to take on the role of customer advocate. Under the new kinetic covenant, workers agree to sign on enthusiastically to the new model and undertake the training that will make them fit for the task. Their quid pro quo: the opportunity to work in a creative, dynamic environment free of bureaucratic frustrations and the chance to share directly in the company's financial successes.

- *Insight:* **Let customer advocates control resources.**

As Pilot Chemicals learned, the more important a customer is to a company, the more he is likely to demand from the relationship—and the more the supplier must be ready to provide. The remarkably swift and effective response by Pilot emerged from its kinetic flexibility. Customer advocates must have the resources at hand that will enable them to satisfy every possible customer need, ranging from strategic to total solutions. That was how Pilot could put together its international account team overnight. There must be networks of experts inside and outside the organization who can respond in real time to an unpredictable challenge.

LET CUSTOMERS PERSONALIZE
THEIR PRODUCTS OR SERVICES

Most companies offer only a handful of product variations. They are based on an organization's past experience, current competition, and a projection of public tastes. When a woman goes shopping for a slip-on shoe, she might have three or four choices: brown or black, with tassels or without, smooth leather or shiny patent. But if her foot is narrower or wider than the average, her choices might actually come down to one.

As we have discussed, customers these days are less and less willing to accept such an arrangement. They want products that, literally and metaphorically, fit their needs. One of the ways the kinetic enterprise makes that possible is by offering a wide array of possible permutations and combinations of the product, so wide that workers can meet virtually any customer's demands.

When it comes to personalizing products or services, the pace is being set by Custom Foot, a shoe store in Westport, Connecticut; a cancer treatment center; and a health care company in Boston. These businesses make it possible for customers to personalize their products or services through technology, supplier and partner connections, customer advocates, and teamwork.

CUSTOM FOOT

Custom Foot gives customers something like two million choices—what amounts to an infinite selection of shoes.

Here's how a customer event transpires at Custom Foot: A customer walks into a retail store that has no inventory. The customer advocate measures the customer's foot in 12 different ways, using an electronic scanner, and then takes the customer on a computer-screen tour of available styles, colors, leathers, linings, soles, and heels. The customer's selections lead to a three-dimensional view of her new shoe, courtesy of specialized software marketed by Trilogy. The order is then translated into Italian and electronically dispatched to shoemakers in Italy.

Within three weeks the customer receives the order, paying an average of $180 a pair for shoes that normally would take several months to make at a cost of up to $1,200.

Are customer-designed shoes the wave of the future? Custom Foot posted sales of about $10 million last year.

THE CANCER TREATMENT CENTER

To maintain its reputation for research and specialized treatment, the center needed to attract patients with the rarest and most recalcitrant forms of cancer. But patients encountered lengthy waits for appointments and were often bounced from specialist to specialist before the right expert was located. Even then, and despite all the previous diagnostic testing, the chosen expert would inevitably order new tests, leading to more appointments and further delay. What's more, communication among the various experts was hit or miss. Patients were often left out of appropriate research programs because the researchers were unaware of the characteristics of patients being seen by their colleagues. "They provide great care if you can only get into the system," one patient commented.

To counter the chaos, the center redesigned itself:

• A toll-free number was established to handle calls from patients and referring physicians. PCs connected to caller I.D. displayed history, accuracy, typical referral, and diagnoses of patients even before a call was answered. Workers operating the phone center immediately assign patients to a care manager.

• A new position was created, that of care manager, to serve as a customer advocate for each patient. Before the first visit, the care manager speaks with the patient at home, obtaining diagnostic information and scheduling any additional tests needed to pinpoint the patient's condition. Familiarity with the organization's cancer specialists and research programs allows the care manager to assign patients to the medical team best suited to their unique forms of cancer.

• Specialists were reassigned from departments to multidisciplinary teams that organized according to the location of patients' cancers. Thus, radiation oncologists, surgical oncologists, and medical oncologists who focus on lung cancer now work together as a team and can provide complete and personalized service for individual patients with lung diseases.

At the center, the care managers/customer advocates shepherd each patient through a personalized medical program. And the increased research population attracted by this kinetic change gives more patients access to innovative care and strongly supports the center's ability to conduct leading-edge research.

BOSTON HEALTH CARE COMPANY

For a patient out in the world, away from hospitals and other treatment centers, life is one long uncertainty. If he has a cardiac problem, for example, and experiences new symptoms or symptoms he knows to be danger signs, he has a hard time knowing just how serious the problem is. Should he reach out to his doctor, which may take hours, or call for a taxi, an ambulance, or a relative to drive him to the emergency room?

A Boston company has developed a twenty-four-hour nursing hotline to help cardiac patients in times of need. The system includes a device that enables cardiac patients to perform an EKG on themselves in their own homes rather than have it done by an intern in the hospital emergency room. The results are then electronically transmitted over the telephone line to nurses and a cardiologist on duty twenty-four hours a day. They have immediate access to the patient's records and can determine whether he should be transported to a hospital. If the patient does need to go to the hospital, the nurse/customer advocate dispatches a specially trained ambulance team. At the same time she notifies the hospital of the incoming patient's exact condition.

Thus, the company provides the patient with a safety net service exactly tailored to his or her needs. A matter of some interest to the patient's insurance company, the service also eliminates unnecessary hospital admissions and emergency room visits.

- *Insight:* **Personalize through technology.**

In the case of Custom Foot, technology allows customers to personally "assemble" their perfect shoe from the virtually un- limited choices the company makes digitally available. Once a design is complete, the data is instantaneously dispatched to shoemakers abroad. The wiring of customers and suppliers yields lightning-fast turnaround.

In the case of the Boston health care company, its technol- ogy allows for personalized service instead of reliance on one- way, standard service centers such as emergency rooms and doctors' offices. The company wires customers at home to de- termine what service is needed: a home remedy or a trip to the emergency room.

- *Insight:* **Personalize through suppliers and partners.**

Under the old mass-market system, any effort to provide prod- ucts to meet customers' infinitely diverse tastes would fall of its own weight. Such an endeavor would require mammoth warehouses filled to the rafters with inventory. The kinetic en- terprise achieves that end, in part, by employing suppliers that can guarantee just-in-time, made-to-order goods. In our Custom

Foot example, the network of shoemakers in Italy is so organized that every individual order from Custom Foot ends with
the delivery of a finished, one-of-a-kind shoe in record time.

The Boston health care company joined with partners—
the ambulance company and the hospital emergency team—to
provide personalized care. Nurses at the twenty-four-hour hotline were wired to ambulance teams and the emergency room
to advise medical professionals concerning the patient's exact
condition.

• *Insight:* **Personalize through customer advocates.**

Traditional organizations provide service in a linear, step-by-
step manner. As our cancer treatment center example shows,
that often confuses and frustrates customers. Patients are passed
from one physician to another, tests are repeated, and there is a
sense that no one knows the whole picture. The kinetic alternative is provided by customer advocates or, as the cancer center
has it, care managers. They know the organization's resources,
and they know where to send the customer/patient to obtain
just what he or she needs without repetitions and delays.

• *Insight:* **Personalize through teamwork.**

Traditional companies organize their human resources according to bureaucratic considerations or, as in our cancer center example, according to the particular specialties of the men
and women involved—surgeons on one floor, as it were, nurses
or aides on another. Kinetic companies organize their resources

to best accommodate the unpredictable demands of their customers, one at a time. They rely on multidiscipline teams that can gather and focus totally on each new customer event. At the cancer center that means organizing resources according to the location of the patient's particular disease, with care handled by a team of expert collaborators.

LET CUSTOMERS INVENT NEW PRODUCTS AND SERVICES

For some corporate customers, a personalized product—be it John Deere's six million-plus possible configurations for a customized seed planter or Custom Foot's two-million-plus possible configurations for a custom-made pair of shoes—is still not enough. These companies need something totally new, a product or service they must have to maintain a competitive edge. Sometimes they call for a new part from a partner so they can launch a breakthrough product. Sometimes internal changes fostered by a reengineering project lead them to ask a supplier for a completely new product or service.

By and large these organizations will be the market pioneers. The more business a company does with them, the more unpredictable their demands on the company are going to be. And that's the good news. By organizing to let such customers drive invention, the company can keep its workers, and the enterprise as a whole, at the leading edge of its industry. The company profits from the sale of the new products or new parts to the demanding customer. And its new expertise enables the company to profit again by selling similar new products to other corporate customers.

In most corporations today, engineering, manufacturing, and logistics experts work in the background, focused on their daily tasks of designing and manufacturing products for their own organization. In a kinetic enterprise such backroom experts become customer advocates, directly responding to customers' unpredictable demands for brand-new products and services.

For most people that represents a major shift in thinking. Suddenly they must learn to see themselves as extensions of the customer, putting the potential needs of the customer and perhaps the customer's customer at the top of their agendas.

Customer advocates must possess a high degree of skill at team play. They must not only be able to work as members of a diversified customer event team but must also know how to help the team get launched quickly and how to help dismantle it. They have to balance the concurrent demands of the several teams on which they serve, all working on short time cycles. What's more, customer advocates must be prepared to design manufacturing and business processes alongside players with whom they have not worked before. They must be prepared to identify suppliers, specialized design experts, and manufacturing partners.

To obtain workers capable of fulfilling this role, companies must invest heavily in training for team innovation and learning. Feedback on how well people operate in a team environment is mandatory.

When it comes to enabling customers to invent new products

and services, G&F Industries and Hewlett-Packard set the pace by commingling operations and dedicating teams to invention.

G&F INDUSTRIES

For G&F Industries of Sturbridge, Massachusetts, the demand for innovation came from the Bose Corporation, which makes high-end stereo systems for homes and automobiles. G&F supplies Bose with plastic components.

A few years ago Bose ran into an unexpected expense in the manufacture of a new speaker cabinet in Japan. The problem was tossed into the lap of Chris LaBonte, a G&F production and inventory control manager who had been assigned to work full-time at Bose headquarters.

The job called for painting, finishing, and assembling a product unlike any G&F had previously built. But LaBonte pledged his company's support and took on the job.

What Bose wanted—a cabinet finished with a thin red stripe—sounded simple enough, but it actually required G&F to invent an entirely new product. Since the stripe could not be painted on, G&F came up with a red frame situated inside the cabinet to create the stripe. The solution won its customer's eternal gratitude.

HEWLETT-PACKARD

A decade ago Ford Motor Company called on the Hewlett-Packard sales team in Detroit and presented a not-so-modest proposal. Ford asked the company to create a new system to detect and diagnose problems with computer-controlled engine parts. Instead of the existing main computer at Ford dealerships, the customer wanted individual diagnostic systems on wheels that could be rolled wherever needed.

Not only did HP produce the mobile units, but it invented a service structure to support Ford dealers using the units around the country. An 800-number hotline was set up, and HP guaranteed that its service workers would be available within two hours of receiving a call no matter where problems cropped up.

Ford next wanted to develop a portable diagnostic system. Often a Ford owner would take the car in for service, complaining about strange noises or performance problems when the car was in motion. HP developed a portable vehicle analyzer as part of the diagnostic system. It needed to be the size of a bread box, sit on the front seat of the car, and plug into the cigarette lighter so that the problem could be diagnosed as the service technician drove the car to duplicate the customer's experience. Once again, HP came through.

What makes this kind of track record possible is a special group within the company called the Integrated Systems Division. It is dedicated to responding to customer requests from anywhere within the organization or directly from customers, and it is staffed by experts of every variety, from sales to R&D to manufacturing to supply-chain management. For each customer request an HP team meets with customer representatives to identify their needs. Then the team builds a prototype, estimates the cost of manufacturing the product, and crafts a plan that will provide a handsome profit for both the customer and HP.

- *Insight:* **Commingle operations.**

Market pioneers are always trying new strategies, inventing new products, and designing new ways to operate so that they can stay in the lead. That puts maximum pressure on suppliers to innovate as well if they want to stay in the game.

To keep up, customer advocates must get as close to such customers as possible. You can't get much closer than G&F and Chris LaBonte got to Bose, and when the customer found itself with a problem, LaBonte was Johnny-on-the-spot.

Nor was LaBonte simply a convenient messenger. Everyone at G&F, frontline and back-office workers alike, was committed to coinventing with their customer, staying abreast of, and participating in, Bose's shifting strategies and product R&D. To make it all happen, G&F workers adopted their customer's goals and operated as part of their customer's virtual enterprise.

- *Insight:* **Dedicate teams to invention.**

How can companies mobilize to meet the unpredictable, daunting challenges so often posed by their best corporate customers? The HP model calls for multidisciplinary teams dedicated to inventing new products for customers old and new. Team members follow kinetic principles, serving as customer advocates; they have amassed an amazing track record for designing and manufacturing new products.

The relationship between Ford and HP is typical of the strong partnerships that kinetic organizations forge with their customers. As the needs of the customer swing with the times, the kinetic supplier is constantly upgrading its own expertise in order to accommodate those needs. HP followed that practice in its pursuit of answers for Ford, not only evolving its technological savvy but spinning off a whole new generation of products on its own.

LET CUSTOMERS DESIGN TOTAL SOLUTIONS

The ultimate kinetic experience is the mobilization necessary to produce a total solution demanded by a single customer. For example, imagine that as a distributor of health care supplies you have received a request for a proposal from your largest customer, a chain of fifty hospitals. The customer wants the supply business bid in a completely new way.

Instead of quoting the cost of the individual items you supply, as is traditional, your customer wants you to provide an estimate for the complete package of supplies, including pharmaceuticals, needed during a patient's entire hospital stay, and the customer wants the estimate for every category of illness. The customer also wants you to take over management of the in-house inventory and deliver products to each of the hospital's patient care units on a just-in-time basis.

Total-solution customer events require customer advocates to create new mini-organizations that tap whatever resources are necessary, both within and outside their ranks. In this instance the supply company's customer advocate would build a team that included a pharmaceutical firm, an organization specializing in on-site inventory management, and a handful of medical consultants to help group the supplies and pharmaceuticals needed for each illness. The team would bid the total solution. If it won, it would enter into a whole new business with built-in profit potential. And even if it were to lose, the supply company would be energized by the bidding process, acquiring new expertise that will enable it to better meet the next unpredictable customer demand.

A customer's total solution often demands products and services that the company does not provide and internal expertise that it does not have on hand. It represents a tremendous challenge to workers to undertake projects they have never experienced. Because of this heightened level of risk-taking, workers need to believe that they will be supported for championing and piloting total-solution events. The building of that trust is one of the major tasks of the kinetic leadership team.

Kinetic companies must also prepare workers to team up with other companies and even support the customer's use of competitive products. Workers need to understand not only what customers need and want but also what suppliers and competitors are doing in the marketplace. Only then will the workers appreciate the necessity of joining forces with those who were, or perhaps still are, competitors or vendors to pursue a total solution.

Who is setting the pace when it comes to letting customers design total solutions? UtiliCorp. How? By partnering with outside experts.

UTILICORP

With the advent of deregulation, utility companies are no longer limited to a single service, such as gas or electric. The individual pieces of the industry devoted to generating, transporting, and marketing energy—kept separate and distinct by regulation—are free to invade each other's turf or branch out into entirely new territory.

UtiliCorp, formerly Missouri Public Service Co., is showing the way. UtiliCorp first marketed its plans for total energy solutions under the name EnergyOne. Then it teamed with PECO Energy, AT&T, and ADT to provide customers with natural gas, electric, telephone, Internet, home security, and energy management services, all from the one source.

In the kinetic future, UtiliCorp will most likely have a telecommunications link to a computer in the customer's house or business that reads the usage meter, optimizes electricity consumption, detects imminent failures in appliance motors before they actually occur, and alerts security personnel to intruders. Home media appliances—televisions, telephones, and personal computers—will let the customer order pay-per-view movies, request new services, or customize the monthly invoice.

In coming years the company will rethink everything from its customer advocates to the way it bills customers and the way it organizes its service infrastructure. One possibility: A complete range of services will be triggered in a single home visit or with a single customer telephone call.

- *Insight:* **Partner with other companies.**

To prepare for total-solution events, the organization must accept the fact that it will not have in-house all of the resources needed. It must be ready to become partners with other individuals and companies, some of whom may even be competitors in other contexts. Witness UtiliCorp's arrangement with PECO Energy, AT&T, and ADT. In the past, suppliers have depended on purchases by repeat customers. Suppliers need to understand that customers' loyalty is best cemented by becoming an integral part of their enterprise. Total solutions make it possible to redefine and extend this business scope while at the same time gaining long-term partner status with customers.

The day is fast approaching when companies will no longer be able to say to their corporate customers or to individual consumers, "Here's our product. These are its features. This is the price list. Take it or leave it." Customers are being conditioned to expect much more, and they will get it.

This will happen, in part, because of the power of the customer events. But it will also depend on the second major element of our design: the market event. It is in these initiatives that the innovative genius of the kinetic enterprise reaches its full flower, as we shall see in the following chapter.

CHAPTER 10

THE FIFTH PATH

IGNITE MARKET EVENTS

While competitors play catch-up, kinetic pioneers create products, services, and businesses that customers and competitors haven't even imagined. Here's how.

INNOVATION with customer events isn't enough to win in today's unpredictable environment. To stay on top, workers must invent new products, services, and businesses that neither customers nor competitors have imagined. Doing so, they create discontinuities that force competitors to change or perish. In a market event, workers strive to invent the future of their enterprise.

The event begins when the active, inquiring mind of a worker spots an opportunity. It takes wing as the worker forms an ad hoc team of colleagues to pursue and refine the idea and realize its potential. They make it happen. They create new ways to operate. They develop new products and services. They innovate with suppliers, partners, and competitors. They invent new businesses.

SEIZE OPPORTUNITIES TO REINVENT OPERATIONS

This is the way twentieth-century companies have always done business: Corporate leaders and their top aides painstakingly set out to predict an industry's future, and create and implement a business design to match the results. They charge their workers with carrying out the design while continuously improving the speed and profitability of the particular process to which they are assigned.

By way of contrast, in a kinetic enterprise, leaders recognize that predictions and cast-in-concrete business designs are irrelevant in today's business climate. In this catch-as-catch-can world, leaders reorganize operations to make it possible to react differently and effectively to various kinds of circumstances. In the new model, the workers do the reacting, and the new operations transfer the initiative to the workers. Rather than simply polishing their current skills, workers become responsible for finding new ways in which they can work together to satisfy single customers in zero time.

Several companies are setting the pace and freeing workers to reinvent operations. Two of the leaders are John Deere and a toy manufacturer we'll call Toy, Inc.

JOHN DEERE

While the team at the Deere Moline plant was setting up its new site—a worker achievement we described in chapter 1—a tool-and-die maker named Ed Hostens was sidelined with an arm injury. But after two months at home he was bored and ready for a new challenge. So he called on his operations manager, Bob Mays, and volunteered to help with the operations transformation.

Hostens accepted a two-month assignment: find ways to quickly change punch press dies. By slashing the time it took to switch from one punch press operation to another, Deere could more profitably produce customized planters, the seed-planting tools attached to tractors.

Soon Hostens was traveling the country, visiting a Chrysler plant, among others, to study tool-and-die techniques and attending conventions and seminars on the topic. And whether he wanted to take a trip or pilot a new approach in the factory, he recalls, "I don't think the company ever told me no. I just approached the person with the checkbook, made the case, got the purchase order, and that was it." Deere outlined the assignment and got out of the way. "They didn't want to limit me with preconceived notions," Hostens says.

Hostens devised a way to alter the dies, rigging them so that the gauging on the die would rise or fall with the push of a lever. By combining the actions of several levers, it became possible to adjust a single die to form different parts. Work that used to require one hundred dies now took only five. Deere managers were ecstatic, and Hostens was assigned to apply his innovation throughout the factory.

After retooling operations at the Moline plant, Hostens shared his new knowledge with manufacturing colleagues from all parts of Deere at one of the technical conferences sponsored periodically by the company. Workers at the sessions compare

notes on what Hostens calls *"Star Wars* gadgets," such as ro-
botics and lasers. Though Hostens felt out of place at first
before this audience composed predominantly of people with
advanced degrees, he soon recovered, and eventually he fielded
more questions than any other speaker. For Hostens, a two-
month assignment turned into a two-year initiative that led to a
significant change in the corporation's ability to execute events
for a single customer in close to zero time.

TOY, INC.

A year or so ago, a woman we know accepted a position in the
customer service department of a large toy manufacturer we will
call Toy, Inc. It didn't take her long to realize that customer
service representatives were responding to complaints without
making full use of the information they were logging into their
computers. When a customer called to say a toy had broken, the
customer service representative simply refunded the customer's
purchase price or sent a new toy. That was the end of it. Case
closed. No questions asked. No information gathered.

Our friend recognized that customer service could participate directly in product innovation. Because Toy, Inc., encouraged workers to ignore traditional job titles and chains of
command, she was able to assemble a temporary team to create
a system for routing complaints directly to the product developers and marketers responsible for particular toys. With the advice and consent of a variety of workers whose help she enlisted,
she also set up a system whereby the newly designed toys, which
incorporated customers' suggestions, were automatically mailed

to complaining customers. Then, to close the loop, service representatives contacted these customers for their critiques of the new, improved toys they received.

Just by keeping her eyes and mind open, our friend was able to initiate and champion a market event that transformed angry customers into long-lasting boosters by including them in the design process.

At Toy, Inc., no "boss" had to sign off on her ideas. In fact, management holds all workers responsible for coming up with such events, continually improving and even reinventing the way they work. That's the job.

- *Insight:* **Give workers access to the information they need to be kinetic.**

Organizations like Toy, Inc., continuously inform workers— through meetings, newsletters, and the Internet—of why they must reinvent operations to satisfy every customer and how to go about it. Workers are regularly provided with relevant data about why customers buy or how purchase patterns affect the value of company stock.

- *Insight:* **Prepare workers to redesign operations.**

At Toy, Inc., workers prepared for events by participating in a variety of reengineering projects. During those years, a designated team captured what workers learned about designing and implementing new processes and new computer systems. For example, they learned that "visioning" sessions proved effective with creative toy designers but were pooh-poohed by rule-oriented financial types. The team then created training classes to transfer the learning to their colleagues, in the form of methods, tools, and techniques. As a result, Toy, Inc.'s workers can think and act like consultants as they seize opportunities to reinvent operations.

- *Insight:* **Give workers authority to make the case for change.**

When market events require significant investment, workers themselves are expected to prepare the business case and compete for corporate funds. They know the facts better than anyone else, and effectively championing their ideas with managers or with the CEO and board of directors is part of their job description. Senior management's role is to motivate and educate so that workers will have an owner's mind-set and want to pursue the event. After that, management should simply get out of the way.

- *Insight:* **Give workers outrageous goals.**

In market events, kinetic workers routinely outperform the old-time preconceptions of what frontline people can accomplish. In a traditional organization there is no way that a factory floor tool-and-die maker like Hostens is going to pursue so outrageous a goal as Mays set for him. It would have gone to an engineering whiz, on orders of the vice president for technology.

But make no mistake: Outrageous goals are not pep-talk pabulum but a practical working element of the kinetic paradigm.

- *Insight:* **Give workers freedom to take risks.**

We have spoken often in these chapters about the hands-off imperative: Senior managers must learn to entertain and support market events without anyone's being—the worker pilot included—all that sure as to where it will end up. In our example, Ed Hostens basically embarked on a fishing expedition, all expenses paid, including visits to pioneering companies. In his case it paid off. It often will not—except insofar as it supports the individual and corporate learning curve and gives credence to the kinetic corporate culture.

SEIZE OPPORTUNITIES TO INVENT
NEW RELATIONSHIPS, PRODUCTS, AND SERVICES

By and large, customers know what kind of relationship they want to have with a company and what kind of products and services are needed for their individual tastes. In the kinetic world, customer advocates are dedicated to responding to these demands, one customer at a time, through the actions we call customer events.

The shoe is on the other foot in market events, in which workers are responsible for spotting opportunities and for inventing relationships, products, and services to exploit them.

Who is setting the pace?

VISTAKON, INC.

Back in 1988 this Johnson & Johnson subsidiary, a manufacturer of specialty contact lenses, had sales of $13 million a year. Its dependence on a single product line—a lens for people with astigmatism—was inhibiting growth. The solution to its problems came from an unexpected direction, in the form of a telephone call from a Danish salesman with a European Johnson & Johnson subsidiary, Janssen Pharmaceutica, to Hank Green, Vistakon's president. The salesman had heard that a Copenhagen ophthalmologist had developed a method for making soft contact lenses, and he thought Vistakon would want to know about it.

Traditionally, soft-lens manufacturing demands that lenses be machined while still hard, then softened in water, a process that can compromise lens accuracy. The Copenhagen ophthalmologist had found a way to mold the lenses in their soft state. Green boarded a plane and within three weeks acquired patent rights to the technology.

It took Vistakon four years to develop the new manufacturing technique and adapt it to low-cost mass production. When it did, the company developed an entirely new lens category around its manufacturing expertise. Today, its Acuvue lens is the leader in the fast-growing disposable contact lens segment.

• *Insight:* **Help workers stay abreast of industry trends.**

The overseas telephone call that put Vistakon on the right track was a surprise, but it was not an accident. Kinetic workers are expected to have a company-wide horizon. They keep abreast of new developments within and outside their own areas of interest, looking for news that could affect their company and its partners.

Kinetic organizations support this search by providing workers with unlimited access to the Internet, by underwriting subscriptions to journals, and by urging workers to attend appropriate conferences. Market events grow out of workers' understanding of their companies' markets.

- *Insight:* **Help workers on every level lead from the front line.**

In the business world of the past, presidents and CEOs issued the orders and their aides implemented them. Leaders were protected from the rough and tumble, and the down-to-earth data that come with encounters on the front line. In our example, Green did not automatically refuse to speak to a "mere" salesman and pass the Danish worker on down the line. He talked to the man himself. Nor did he dispatch a team of lawyers to nail down the patent on the new soft lens manufacturing technique and assign his engineering vice president to pursue the project. He recognized the potential importance of this strategic opportunity, and he became the pilot and champion of an event that eventually turned his company around.

In the kinetic world, leaders are part of the team. They are accessible to their workers. They are available to help solve intractable problems or to clinch a sale with a personal visit. They do not lead from on high but from the front line.

SEIZE OPPORTUNITIES TO INNOVATE
WITH SUPPLIERS, PARTNERS, AND COMPETITORS

In their search for market event opportunities and in their pursuit of opportunities found, kinetic leaders and other workers recognize their limits. They understand that collaboration, so vital to the operations of their own organization, can also be applied outside, that by cooperating directly with suppliers and partners they can unlock the unrecognized potential of a market event.

At an office furniture manufacturer, a purchasing manager stays close to a partner who is developing new lightweight lumbar-support systems. He hopes to coinvent a new generation of chairs. At a latex glove manufacturer, a sales representative has an occasional lunch with a research manager at a chemical company. Her aim is to keep up with the latest developments in latex substitutes.

Our research shows that Infonet, formerly a division of Computer Sciences Corporation, and John Deere are setting the pace when it comes to collaborating with suppliers, partners, and even competitors.

INFONET

When the United States deregulated data communications in the middle 1980s, Infonet entered the very confused data networking business. At that point there was no set of commonly accepted definitions of the basic elements of the industry. Then one of Infonet's scientists persuaded the company to help finance the efforts of a newly formed industry group that was hoping to set global standards for data networking.

It was the beginning of a market event. The scientist understood that cooperation with competitors was in a good cause if it could lead to new industry-wide definitions, because they would make it possible for Infonet to launch new networking products and services.

As part of the standard-setting process, each member of the group shared his or her company's most promising technologies. One company, for example, contributed its addressing protocol; another, its encryption technology. The market event ended when Infonet rolled out its new line of networking services.

JOHN DEERE

Outward-bound collaboration is part of the drill at Deere's Moline facility, and Bud Young has learned the lesson well. Young assembles parts from several suppliers into something called a finger pickup unit, a device that picks up seeds and deposits them in the soil. When he found that one of the parts contained a small defect, he did not—as he might have in years past—report the problem to his supervisor. Nor did he contact one of the supplier's managers. Instead, he picked up a telephone and called a frontline worker at the supplier company and arranged for the man to meet him at his Deere workstation. Once the supplier's worker observed the flaw in the part firsthand, he went back to his plant and immediately saw to it that the necessary changes were made. Simultaneous collaborations like this enable workers to catch and fix quality problems before they reach the customer, enabling Deere to market and consistently deliver high-quality customized products.

- *Insight:* **Allow workers to make connections.**

Nobody at Deere told Young what to do when he had trouble with a supplier's work. In traditional companies he would automatically have called over his foreman. At Deere, workers are expected to exercise initiative and use their own judgment. That is the essence of the new covenant with workers.

- *Insight:* **Allow workers to cross boundaries.**

The Infonet worker who convinced company leaders of the importance of collaborating with competitors to create industry standards was a scientist, not a marketing analyst or an executive planner. In a kinetic organization, workers in every corner of the enterprise are responsible for spotting and championing market event ideas and for considering all potential partners, even their competitors.

- *Insight:* **Allow workers to pursue ideas.**

If workers are to initiate market events, as at Deere and Infonet, they need to be aware of what's happening in their own and allied industries. The new ideas can be found in newsletters and journals, to be sure, but they tend to crop up first in informal discussions at industry meetings. That's why it is essential that a substantial number of workers be actively involved in their trade associations. To a degree far greater than is true of traditional organizations, new ideas are the lifeblood of a kinetic corporation.

SEIZE OPPORTUNITIES TO INVENT NEW BUSINESSES

Employees of high-tech organizations are notorious for jumping ship to start their own businesses. No salary is going to match the potential bonanza that the founder of a company can realize.

Some companies view market events as breeding grounds for start-ups. They use the events to engage workers in building and leading new businesses, and then spin the new enterprises off as independent partner companies.

THERMO ELECTRON CORPORATION

The 1996 annual report of the Thermo Electron Corporation of Waltham, Massachusetts, features twenty men and women on its fold-out cover. Each of them is shown proclaiming, "I'm the CEO." And so they are—of businesses that have been spun off the parent company.

In the report, George Hatsopoulos, founder and, yes, CEO of the $3 billion concern, asks, "Why do we have so many CEOs?" His answer: "Because we . . . want to encourage entrepreneurship and innovation. . . . Our basic philosophy maintains that a company can only perpetuate itself in the long run by exploring new businesses. . . . Our structure provides one-stop shopping for entrepreneurs. Nobody ever has to leave Thermo Electron to become a great start-up success. They can start their own companies right here."

At the moment, twenty-one spinouts (and spinouts of spinouts) orbit the parent company. These publicly traded, stand-alone companies are in such businesses as environmental and analytical instruments, cogeneration systems, process equipment, biomedical devices, specialty materials, and metallurgical services. Within Thermo the various divisions compete constantly to become the next spinout. To be cut loose they must demonstrate the potential to grow a minimum of 30 percent a year.

Thermo holds on to a majority stake in each spinout but gives day-to-day control and enormous numbers of stock options to workers in each new enterprise. In most instances the spinouts, not Thermo itself, pocket the proceeds when shares are sold to the public. Thermo does, however, receive "a gain on issuance of stock by subsidiaries"—that is, the difference between the book value and the price of minority stakes.

Thermo provides spinouts with a wide range of assistance, including financial, legal, tax, human resources, and public relations services. It also maintains a central research division that enables technical people from all over the enterprise to work jointly on new products. The parent company in return collects from each spinout a fee of 1 percent of its annual revenues.

In addition, Thermo provides its name to spinouts, making it easier for them to attract investors and customers. To further strengthen the connections between Thermo and its spinouts, stock options are usually split so that 40 percent is tied to the performance of a particular spinout, 40 percent to Thermo's performance, and 20 percent to the performance of all other spinouts.

• *Insight:* **Provide a compelling strategic purpose.**

A kinetic company's strategic purpose is not just for show—it drives the whole enterprise. Thermo Electron might have chosen as its strategic purpose "to make the world's best environmental analysis equipment" or "to be to the environmental industry what Microsoft is to computer software." Instead it focused on what its leaders perceived as their true mission: to explore and generate new businesses, wherever that might lead the organization. As its string of spinoff companies demonstrates, Thermo Electron has consistently adhered to its strategic purpose, and prospered mightily in the process.

• *Insight:* **Provide strong entrepreneurial support.**

To achieve success in creating new businesses, kinetic organizations should establish a wide variety of entrepreneurial services to help the fledglings fly. The workers who pilot these ultimate market events need all the expertise they can marshal.

That goes in spades when the organization is considering spinning off the new business on its own. In the case of Thermo Electron, the services provided by the parent company range from financial to public relations to research. They take some of the risk out of the company's bet on its aspiring entrepreneurs, who are all too eager to fly. What Thermo Electron wants to prevent at all costs is the distinct possibility that the best and brightest of its talent will leave the nest.

We have just about completed our armchair journey toward the kinetic enterprise. It has taken us into some unlikely corners of the business world, from a TV station with no stage sets to the back of a hospital-bound ambulance. We have explored industries as disparate as manufacturers of farm tractors and windows, supermarkets, and health care providers. In almost every case, though, the lens of our mind's eye has had an unusual focus: We have sought those moments when the organizations have gone kinetic.

The analogy to sports is too tempting to resist. When a Michael Jordan or a Jerry Rice or a Tiger Woods is operating full-out, achieving and surpassing his potential, we say he is in the zone. When an enterprise organized around kinetic principles comes to grips with a customer demand or a market opportunity, when a team of workers immediately forms to organize the right response and pursues it to a profitable ending, then we say that this company, too, is in the zone.

As we have seen, the true power of the kinetic model lies in its capacity to succeed under circumstances that put traditional companies out of business, when markets can no longer be predicted with any degree of accuracy and confidence—in other words, the circumstances that now exist in many markets and are becoming commonplace around the developed world. This book was born out of our belief that we must all find a new way to do business and that kinetics offers that way.

We also feel that the kinetic enterprise has a significance that goes beyond the confines of the business world. A word about that is presented in the epilogue.

EPILOGUE

As you may remember, we started this book by suggesting that you sometimes have to "step back a minute" from the customary pressures and challenges of your life in order to make sense of it. All those trees have a way of obscuring the forest—that's what we said. But then we realized that we had ignored our own advice.

We have spelled out at length the urgent need to prepare for the onrushing world of unpredictability and the ways in which kinetics can accomplish that end. We have described how you can start applying the principles of kinetics in your business, following the examples of dozens of enterprises that have begun to achieve significant new advantage by doing so.

What we have failed to convey is the thrill and excitement of a transparent kinetic business environment, a workplace where everyone is joined in a common frontline campaign; where differences of rank and status are virtually wiped away; where the long-hidden spirit of adventure and innovation in all of us can finally gain free rein.

We are businesspeople, not sociologists or psychologists, but we do believe that once the kinetic model gains wide acceptance, it will fundamentally change the nature of work. And that, in turn, is certain to have a profound effect on the society as a whole.

In the traditional business setting, most workers are replaceable cogs in the bureaucratic machine, taking and giving orders according to an old and rigid set of rules and boundaries. Their jobs and the way the jobs are done are preordained. We learn early not to rock the boat, not to take chances, and our connections with our colleagues are often more competitive than collaborative. To be sure there are exceptions to this dismal picture —individuals and organizations do sometimes rise above the system—but it is difficult, to say the least.

All that is forever altered by kinetics. In an enterprise that thrives on customer and market events, success depends entirely on the ability of individual workers to maintain and exploit their connections with colleagues. Collaboration is not a feel-good goal but the essential engine of the enterprise. Workers are expected to engage in creative risk-taking, not because it is a liberating activity but because it is a key element of the kinetic design. Their commitment to the organization's larger goals reflects their new responsibilities and their new ownerlike relationship to the enterprise.

Consider for a moment the emotional impact of the kinetic environment on some of the workers we have discussed in this book. That copy-machine operator at Kinko's, for example, who thought up the custom calendar. He developed the product, reported its local success to CEO Paul Orfalea by voice mail, and saw his idea spread throughout the organization. Imagine his excitement and sense of personal fulfillment, and how that kind of experience can energize and motivate workers.

Or imagine how workers are inspired when a CEO like Martin Goldsmith of the Albert Einstein Healthcare Network puts himself on the line. During the redesign of his institution, you may recall, Goldsmith invited criticism, was told he would have to become more team-oriented, among other things, and proceeded to change his ways. Leading from the front line, presenting himself as a role model, he inspired a wholehearted, enthusiastic response.

The kinetic transformation of businesses and workers seems certain to change some basic attitudes within our culture. The emphasis on personal collaboration instead of competition, for example, and on individual initiative rather than order-taking, will surely be reflected in our educational system as well as our mores. So will the kinetic demand for continual learning.

There have been many studies of the harm caused by the built-in stresses of the assembly line, on the one hand, and the corporate ladder, on the other. Dysfunctional workers breed dysfunctional families. But our children and their children are going to experience a vastly different career path, one in which workers on every level and in every corner of the enterprise enjoy the satisfactions of initiating and piloting kinetic events and then sharing in the profits thereof.

The primary focus of this book is, of course, more immediate and pragmatic. We have designed it to be both a spur and a guide: a spur to recognize the permanence of the changes that have torn up our business environment, and a guide to help cope with those changes. We hope that you will heed our warnings and that you will find ways to apply kinetics in your own backyard. As so many enterprises have discovered, the path of kinetics can be difficult and demanding, but the rewards are sure and plentiful.

REFERENCES

"The Ambidextrous Organization," *Journal of Business Strategy,* July/August, 1997.

"Automation Helps AMP Boost Quality, Cut Scrap," *Plastics World,* May, 1997, p. 31.

"Barnes & Noble Opens Richmond, California, Store, Changing America's Concept of the Neighborhood Bookstore," *Business Wire,* May 2, 1997.

Bartlett, Christopher A., and Afroze Mohammed, "3M: Profile of an Innovating Company," *Harvard Business School,* January 3, 1995, pp. 2, 4.

Berry, Leonard L., "Retailers with a Future: Five Benefits Distinguish Companies That Compete on Value," *Marketing Management,* Spring, 1996, p. 38.

Bossidy, Larry, "Larry Bossidy Won't Stop Pushing," *Fortune,* January 13, 1997, pp. 135–36.

Branch, Shelly, "So Much Work, So Little Time," *Fortune,* February 3, 1997, p. 115.

Callebs, Sean, "High Tech Is Making Shopping Fast, Fun, and Easy," *CNN: Your Money,* December 7, 1996, transcript.

Collins, James C., and Jerry I. Porras, *Built to Last: Successful Habits of Visionary Companies* (New York: HarperBusiness, 1994).

Deschamps, Jean-Philippe, and Nayak P. Ranganath, "Fomenting a Customer Obsession: Rubbermaid Inc.'s Product Development Strategy," *National Productivity Review,* September 22, 1995, p. 89.

Dixon, Lance, and Anne Millen Porter, *JIT II: Revolution in Buying & Selling* (Newton, Massachusetts: Cahners Publishing Company, 1994).

Donlon, J. P., "Not By Technology Alone: Interview with Thermo Electron Corp.'s George Hatsopoulos," *ASAP,* April, 1993, p. 38.

Fishman, Charles, "We've Seen the Future of Work and It Works, But Very Differently," *Fast Company,* August/September, 1996, pp. 54–62.

Ford Motor Company Annual Report, 1996.

Freiberg, Kevin, and Jackie Freiberg, *Nuts! Southwest Airlines' Crazy Recipe for Business and Personal Success* (Austin, Texas: Bard Press, 1996).

Gates, Bill, *The Road Ahead* (New York: Viking, 1995).

Gilmore, James H., and B. Joseph Pine II, "The Four Faces of Mass Customization," *Harvard Business Review,* January/February, 1997, p. 99.

Goman, Carol Kinsey, "Energizing a Restructured Work Force," *Communication World,* February, 1997, p. 55.

Gramig, Mickey H., "Coca-Cola a Little Shy of Forecast: 'Currency Hit,' " *The Atlanta Journal–Constitution,* January 29, 1998, p. 1.

Greenwald, John, reported by Wendy Cole-Livonia and William A. McWhirter, "Reinventing Sears," *Time,* December 23, 1996, p. 52.

Grove, Andrew S., *Only the Paranoid Survive: How to Exploit the Crisis Points That Challenge Every Company and Career* (New York: Currency, 1996).

———, "Only the Productive Survive," *Forbes ASAP,* December 1, 1997, p. 22.

Gunther, Marc, "This Gang Controls Your Kids' Brains," *Fortune,* October 27, 1997, p. 172.

Hamel, Gary, and C. K. Prahalad, *Competing for the Future: Breakthrough Strategies for Seizing Control of Your Industry and Creating the Markets of Tomorrow* (Boston: Harvard Business School Press, 1994).

Hammer, Michael, "The Fast Company Unit of One Anniversary Handbook," *Fast Company,* February/March, 1997, p. 102.

Harari, Oren, "Stop Empowering Your People: The Best of Cutting Edge," *Management Review,* February, 1997, p. 48.

Hartman, Curtis, "Sales Force," *Fast Company,* June/July, 1997, p. 146.

Hatsopoulos, George N. "A Perpetual Idea Machine: Thermo Electron Corp.," *ASAP,* March 22, 1996, p. 81.

Holden, Benjamin, "UtiliCorp and PECO, Aided by AT&T, to Launch One-Stop Utility Service," *The Wall Street Journal,* June 24, 1997, p. 3.

Holley, David, "At a Time When Diversification Is Often Suspect, the Japanese Auto Giant, Guided by a Historical Perspective, Is Moving into Other Areas Such as Housing and, Especially, Telecommunications: Toyota Heads Down a New Road," *The Los Angeles Times,* March 16, 1997, p. 1.

Holusha, John, "A New Spirit at U.S. Auto Plants," *The New York Times,* December 29, 1987, p. 1.

Huffaker, Donna, "Wonderbra Sure to Stir Local Interest," *Parkersburg Sentinel,* October 7, 1994, p. 1.

Isaacson, Bruce, "Bose Corporation: The JIT II Program (A)," *Harvard Business School,* March 8, 1994, p. 1.

Kanter, Rosabeth Moss, John Kao, and Fred Wiersema, *BusinessMaster: Innovation* (New York: HarperBusiness, 1997).

Kets de Vries, V. R. Manfred, "The Downside of Downsizing," *Human Relations,* January, 1997, p. 11.

Kim, James, "Windows 98 Grabs the Web: Microsoft Targets Internet Market," *USA Today,* July 24, 1997, p. 1B.

Kirkpatrick, David, "Intel's Amazing Profit Machine," *Fortune,* February 17, 1997, pp. 60, 64.

Labarre, Polly, "This Organization: How Denmark's Oticon Thrives on Chaos," *Fast Company,* June/July, 1996, pp. 110–13.

Littman, Jonathan, "The Book on Amazon.com," *The Los Angeles Times Magazine,* July 20, 1997, pp. 18–28.

Loeb, Marshall, "Ten Commandments for Managing Creative People," *Fortune,* January 16, 1995, pp. 135–36.

Magretta, Joan, "Growth Through Global Sustainability, an Interview with Monsanto's CEO, Robert B. Shapiro," *Harvard Business Review,* January/February, 1997, p. 87.

Martin, Justin, Reporter Associate, Joyce E. Davis, "Are You as Good as You Think You Are?" *Fortune,* September 30, 1996, pp. 142–52.

Matson, Erik, "The Discipline of High-Tech Leaders," *Fast Company,* April/May, 1997, p. 34.

McDermott, Michael J., "Coke and Pepsi: Still at It After All These Years," *Food and Beverage Marketing,* August, 1997, p. 12.

McDonald's Corporation Annual Report, 1996.

McWilliams, Gary, "Whirlwind on the Web," *Business Week,* April 7, 1997, p. 132.

Nartin, Justin, "Give 'Em Exactly What They Want: An Innovative Young Shoe Company Uses a Manufacturing Strategy Worth Watching," *Fortune,* November 10, 1997, p. 283.

Nauss, Donald W., "Ready, Wheeling, and Able—That's AutoNation USA," *The Los Angeles Times,* February 2, 1997, p. 1.

Nee, Eric, "One on One with Eric Nee: Rich McGinn," *Upside,* February, 1997, pp. 82–86.

Nine West Group Annual Report, 1996.

Norwest Corporation Annual Report, 1996.

Novicki, Christina, "Don't Change That Channel . . . Change the Rules!" *Fast Company,* January 20, 1997, p. 87.

"Open Gates," *The Scotsman,* December 4, 1995, p. 12.

Powell, Tom, "Evaluating Sponsor Opportunities Through the Eyes of Sara Lee," *Amusement Business,* June 27, 1994, p. 5.

Power, Christopher, with Joseph Weber, Joan O'C. Hamilton, and Jeffrey Ryser, "At Johnson & Johnson, a Mistake Can Be a Badge of Honor," *Business Week,* September 26, 1988, p. 126.

Reese, Jennifer, "Thermo Electron: How to Grow Big by Staying Small," *Fortune,* December 28, 1992, p. 50.

Rifkin, Glenn, "Nothing But Net," *Fast Company,* June/July, 1996, pp. 122–27.

Sabbagh, Karl, *Twenty-first-Century Jet: The Making and Marketing of the Boeing 777* (New York: Scribner, 1996).

Sauer, Matthew, "AutoNation Steering Toward Sarasota-Bradenton," *Sarasota Herald Tribune,* December 15, 1997, p. 1.

Schonberger, R. J., *Japanese Manufacturing Techniques* (New York: Free Press, 1983).

Sears, Roebuck and Co., Annual Report, 1997.

Sellers, Patricia, "Sears: The Turnaround Is Ending," *Fortune,* April 28, 1997, p. 106.

Serrill, Michael S., "Brazil's Dream Factory—Volkswagen's Futuristic Truck Plant Offers a Radical New Concept: No VW Employee Ever Tightens a Bolt," *Time,* November 11, 1996, p. 35.

Serwer, Andrew E., "Michael Dell Turns the PC World Inside Out," *Fortune,* September 8, 1997, pp. 76–86.

Sheff, David, "Levi's Changes Everything: An Inside Account of the Most Dramatic Change Program in American Business," *Fast Company,* June/July, 1996, pp. 66–74.

Sherman, Stratford, and Anthony Rucci, "Bringing Sears into the New World," *Fortune,* October 13, 1997, p. 183.

Sivy, Michael, Reporter Associate, Jeanhee Kimanalysis, "How to Cash in on the Asian Boom," *Money,* May, 1997, p. 108.

Smart, Tim, with Peter Burrows, "Out to Make Xerox Print More Money," *Business Week,* August 11, 1997, p. 81.

"Spinning It Out at Thermo Electron," *The Economist,* April 12, 1997, p. 57.

Steinhauer, Jennifer, "Time to Call a Sears Repairman," *The New York Times,* January 15, 1997, pp. 1–3.

Stevens, Tim, "And One to Grow On," *Industry Week,* July 3, 1995, p. 27.

Stross, Randall E., "Microsoft's Big Advantage—Hiring Only the Super-smart," *Fortune,* November 25, 1996, pp. 159–62.

———, *The Microsoft Way: The Real Story of How the Company Outsmarts the Competition* (Reading, Massachusetts: Addison-Wesley Publishing Company, Inc., 1996).

———, Reporter Associate, Alicia Hills Moore, "Mr. Gates Builds His Brain Trust," *Fortune,* December 8, 1997, p. 84.

Sullivan, Gordon R., and Michael V. Harper, *Hope Is Not a Method: What Business Leaders Can Learn from America's Army* (New York: Random House, 1996).

Taylor, Alex, "Car Wars: Wayne Huizenga vs. Everybody," *Fortune,* June 9, 1997, p. 92.

Taylor, William C., "At VeriFone It's a Dog's Life (and They Love It!)," *Fast Company,* October/November, 1996, p. 15.

————, "Who's Writing the Book on Web Business?," *Fast Company,* October/November 1996, pp. 132–33.

Thermo Electron Corporation Annual Report, 1996.

Torres, Vicki, "A Hidden High-Tech Hot Spot," *The Los Angeles Times,* December 18, 1996, p. 1A.

Updike, Edith Hill, and Keith Naughton, "Ford Has a Long Haul at Mazda," *Business Week,* October 7, 1996, pp. 108–14.

Utterback, James M., *Mastering the Dynamics of Innovation: How Companies Can Seize Opportunities in the Face of Technological Change* (Harvard Business School Press, 1994).

Walter, John R., "How to Leap Before You Look: Lessons for a Digital World," *The New York Times,* November 10, 1996, p. 12.

Weber, Joseph, "How J&J's Foresight Made Contact Lenses Pay," *Business Week,* May 4, 1992, p. 132.

Wiersema, Fred, *Customer Intimacy* (Santa Monica: Knowledge Exchange, 1996).

Wilson, Ian H., "The Five Compasses of Strategic Leadership," *Strategy & Leadership,* July, 1996, p. 26.

Zwiebach, Elliot, "Nobody Doesn't Like . . . John H. Bryan; CEO of Sara Lee Corp.," *Supermarket News,* May 26, 1986, p. 6.

INDEX

deciding if right for business, 53, 54, 55, 56
developing best approach to, 53, 54–55, 56, 57
exploiting, 25, 36, 37, 161
identification of, 21
responding to, 99
seized by workers, 40
seizing unexpected, 43–60
spotting unexpected, 53–54, 55, 56, 57–58
see also Marshaling resources
Market pioneers, 198–99, 202
Market share, 30, 58
Market shifts, 47–48, 116
Market trends, 16, 35, 115
Marketers, 47, 48
Marketing professionals, 46
Markets, 25, 222
foreign, 35
fragmenting, 183
new, 116, 119
newcomers invading, 30
small, 46
Marshaling resources, 37, 45–46
to capitalize on opportunity, 53, 54, 55–57
to meet customer's demand, 69, 70
Martinez, Arthur C., 38–39, 40
Mass customization, 65
Mass market(s), 63, 171, 184, 196
Mass-market paradigm, 114
Mays, Bob, 209, 212
Mazda Motor Corporation, 17–18
MCI Communications Corporation, 37, 116, 150

MCI Telecommunications, 77–78
performance goals, 77–78
MCI TV, 78
Media conglomerates, 49–52
Medical emergency treatment, 158–160, 161
Medical programs, personalized, 193–96, 197
Melissa Manifesto, 22
Memphis, Tennessee, 87, 88
Mentors, 147
Merrill Lynch & Co., Inc., 24
Micromanagement, 113
Micro-marketing, 65
Microsoft Corporation, 19, 28, 37, 74, 92, 108–09
hiring, 130–31, 133, 134
outrageous customer benefit, 59–60
rewarding enterprise-wide performance, 149
strategic purpose, 118–19
Milstead, Bob, 107–08, 143–44, 173, 174
Mini-organizations, 203–04
Minneapolis, 186
Minnesota Mining and Manufacturing (3M), 22–23, 33, 92, 93–94, 150
Genesis Grants, 105
nurturing collaboration, 87
Missouri Public Service Co., 205
Miyoshi, Susumu, 119
Module team(s), 80
Moline, Illinois, 23, 208, 209, 217
Monitoring mechanisms, 139
Monsanto Company, 29, 71
Morristown, New Jersey, 29

Owners
workers think like, 73–76, 133
Ownership, sense of, 74, 150–51

Pace
old, 30, 33–34
Palo Alto, California, 74
Partner companies/partners, 180,
181, 219
innovation with, 216–19
personalizing through, 192, 196,
198
prequalified, 166
Partnering, 206
on the fly, 166
spontaneous, 165–66
Patton, Paul, 141, 142
Peapod Inc., 30
PECO Energy Company, 31, 205,
206
Pensacola, Florida, 174
Pentium chip, 43
Performance, 98
measurement of, 121
viewing, 170
Performance goals, 101
common, 76–78
Personal communications services,
80–81
Personal computers, 49, 166
in customer event(s), 67–68
files, 162
Kaiser Permanente, 162–64
software, 166, 170
Personalizing products and services,
22, 192–98
PETsMART, Inc., 32
Pharmaceutical, Inc., 168–69, 170

Philadelphia, Pennsylvania, 31
Phoenix, Arizona, 32, 186
Pink Dot Inc., 30
Planter(s), customized, 23–24, 209–
210
Platt, Lewis E., 98–99
Polaroid Corporation, 31
Population trends, 27
Portland, Oregon, 123
Post-it Notes, 33
Prahalad, C. K., 48
Predictability, 27, 28
death of, 15–41
Prediction(s), 25, 208
Problem solving, 81, 84
through networks, 86
Process
companies organized by, 116
Process masters, 85–87
Process technology
to serve single customers, 154,
171–78
Processes, 113, 153
adaptable, 151
Procter & Gamble Company, 35
Product development, 33, 35
Product development team(s), 51
Product managers, 47, 48
Production, 173–74, 175–76
scheduled, 16
units of one, 177
Production runs, 171, 177
Productivity, 36, 153, 164
Products, 25
customized, 22, 24, 209–10, 218,
226
custom-made, 48
customer-designed, 183, 184

ABOUT THE AUTHORS

MICHAEL FRADETTE is a partner with Deloitte Consulting, and is global director of manufacturing management consulting. His areas of expertise include enterprise transformation, supply chain, strategic cost management, manufacturing systems, and factory modernization. He has more than twenty-five years of consulting and industry operating experience in a variety of manufacturing companies in high-technology process, consumer products, and the automotive, aerospace, and defense industries. He lives in Boston.

STEVE MICHAUD is a partner with Deloitte Consulting, and was the founding national director of the firm's Client/Server Solutions service line. Today he is a leader in the firm's Enterprise Applications Systems practice. His areas of expertise include information-technology planning and business-process reengineering, systems integration, and redesigning in-house IT organizations. In two decades of consulting, he has worked with a wide variety of companies, including insurance, health care, real estate, telecommunications, public sector, and professional service firms. He lives in Los Angeles.